TOP 10 SHANGHAI 2025

TRAVEL GUIDE

Gerald E. Priddy

Table Of Contents

Welcome to Shanghai

Welcome to Shanghai, a city that, with its sweeping skyline and rich history, instantly pulls you in. I remember the first time I stepped into this dynamic metropolis, feeling both excited and overwhelmed by the sheer magnitude of everything around me. From the glossy towers of Pudong to the ancient lanes of the Old Town, Shanghai is a place where the past and future meet in a way that's almost magical. As I wandered through its bustling streets, I was struck by how easy it was to get lost in the rhythm of this city, where every corner seemed to hold a new adventure.

My first morning in Shanghai started with a rush of energy—people hurriedly going about their daily routines, the air thick with the scent of street food, and the hum of the city itself. I found myself near the Bund, mesmerized by the iconic skyline and the gentle lapping of the Huangpu River. I couldn't help but think that this was a city that never really stopped, yet it somehow felt inviting and full of life. Walking along the riverbanks, with the city's shining buildings on one side and the quieter, older structures of colonial-era Shanghai on the other, I felt as though I was caught between two worlds.

One of the most striking things about Shanghai is how much it's rooted in its traditions. Even amidst the dazzling lights and modern architecture, there are echoes of history. I took a detour through the narrow alleyways of the Old Town, where the rhythm of everyday life was so different from the glitzy world across the river. The streets were alive with the sounds of vendors shouting out their goods, families sitting down to lunch in tiny restaurants, and the occasional temple bells ringing in the distance. It was here, in these winding alleys, where I discovered a hidden gem—a small tea shop tucked away in a corner, where an elderly woman taught me the art of tea brewing. The stillness of the moment contrasted so beautifully with the bustle just outside.

What I loved most about Shanghai, though, was how it never let me feel like a tourist. Sure, there were the towering shopping malls and the sparkling streets of Nanjing Road, but I found that the best experiences often came from simply observing the city around me. I spent an evening at the famous Yu Garden, one of the city's oldest and most beautiful spots, where I watched locals stroll through its serene paths, all the while savoring the peaceful sounds of the koi ponds and the rustling leaves. And when night fell, I ventured into the lively neighborhoods of Xintiandi and found myself caught up in the evening buzz, with people chatting, laughing, and enjoying the warm night air.

Shanghai is a city that effortlessly blends the old with the new, and I think that's why it captivated me so much. There are pockets of history everywhere you look, from ancient temples to old buildings now standing side-by-side with modern skyscrapers. At the same time, the city is always pushing forward, embracing technology and innovation in ways I had never seen before. I think it's this dynamic energy that makes Shanghai so unique, so impossible to define with just one word.

But more than anything, what I took away from my time in Shanghai was the sense that it is a city that invites you to explore, to get lost, and to be amazed by the layers of history and culture that are woven into every street and building. Whether you're here for the art, the food, the shopping, or just to feel the pulse of a city that never sleeps, Shanghai promises to show you something you'll remember long after you leave. And, just as it did for me, it will likely leave you wanting to return again and again.

So, let me invite you to embark on this journey. Whether it's your first time or your fiftieth, Shanghai has something new to offer, and I can't wait for you to experience it in your own way.

PLANNING YOUR TRIP

Best Time to Visit

When planning your trip to Shanghai, the timing of your visit can make all the difference in shaping your experience. If you're looking to explore this vibrant metropolis under the most pleasant conditions, the best time to go is during the spring, between March and May. During these months, the city comes alive with mild temperatures, ranging from the mid-50s to low 70s (°F), and the air is filled with the sweet scent of blossoms. The city's parks and gardens, such as the beautiful Yu Garden, are adorned in vivid shades of pink, white, and purple, making it the perfect time for leisurely strolls along the Bund or through the city's many tree-lined avenues. Spring also brings a sense of rejuvenation to Shanghai as locals enjoy the moderate weather, making outdoor activities more enjoyable and accessible.

Autumn, from September to November, is another wonderful time to visit Shanghai,
often considered the second-best season after spring. The weather is just as comfortable, with cool, crisp air and plenty of sunshine. The city's skyline gleams against the backdrop of clear skies, and the temperature hovers around the mid-60s to mid-70s (°F), making it ideal for sightseeing and dining at outdoor cafes. Fall is also when many of Shanghai's most iconic events take place, including the popular Shanghai International Arts Festival and numerous food festivals celebrating both local and international cuisines. The fall foliage, while not as dramatic as in some places, still offers a picturesque view, especially in the city's quieter parks like Century Park.

That being said, summer and winter each have their own unique charm, though they come with considerations. Summer in Shanghai, stretching from June to August, can be sweltering, with temperatures often soaring above 90°F (32°C), accompanied by high humidity. The city's bustling energy remains undeterred, but you'll need to take extra care with hydration and seek out air-conditioned venues for comfort. However, this is also when Shanghai offers its best summer festivals, open-air markets, and a lively food scene that comes to life after dark. On the flip side, winter, from December to February, is typically cold and dry, with temperatures dipping into the 30s and 40s (°F). The lack of snow doesn't detract from the festive atmosphere, though, as the city lights up for Chinese New Year celebrations. Winter may not be ideal for outdoor activities, but the cozy ambiance of Shanghai's tea houses and indoor markets more than makes up for the chill in the air.

Getting to Shanghai

When you begin planning your journey to Shanghai, one of China's most dynamic and fast-paced cities, the first step is figuring out how to get there, and there are several options to choose from. The approach you take depends on where you're flying in from and what your travel preferences are. But whether you're hopping on an international flight from across the globe or taking a high-speed train from another Chinese city, getting to Shanghai is part of the adventure, setting the stage for the energy and excitement that awaits in this sprawling metropolis.

If you're traveling internationally, your first stop will likely be Shanghai Pudong International Airport (PVG), which serves as the city's main international gateway. Located about 30 kilometers (19 miles) east of the city center, Pudong is one of the busiest airports in China and an important hub for both domestic and international flights. The airport is well-connected to major cities worldwide, with direct flights from places like New York, London, Tokyo, Paris, and Sydney, to name just a few. Major international airlines such as Emirates, Air France, British Airways, and American Airlines operate flights to and from Shanghai, ensuring there's plenty of choice in terms of comfort and pricing.

Booking a flight to Shanghai can be done through multiple platforms, from online travel agencies to directly through airlines. If you're looking for convenience and competitive prices, websites like Expedia, Skyscanner, and Google Flights are excellent tools to compare different flights, check prices, and determine the best times to fly. On average, a round-trip flight to Shanghai from North America or Europe can range from $600 to $1,500, depending on the time of year, the airline, and how far in advance you book. The general rule is that the earlier you book, the better the prices, but keep in mind that flying during peak seasons like Chinese New Year or the summer months can drive prices higher.

Once you've booked your flight, it's important to note your booking number, which you'll use when checking in or for any inquiries. Your booking number typically appears on your confirmation email, along with flight details and your e-ticket. If you're booking through a travel agency or a third-party website, they'll provide you with all the necessary documentation. If booking directly with an airline, they'll often give you access to a mobile app or a website portal to track your flight and make any necessary adjustments to your itinerary. Some airlines also provide easy-to-use mobile apps that can

give you access to your boarding pass and gate information, making the travel experience smoother once you've arrived at the airport.

When you arrive at Shanghai Pudong International Airport, you'll find that it's an impressive, modern facility with all the amenities you might need, including free Wi-Fi, plenty of restaurants and shopping, and clear signage in both Chinese and English. For transportation into the city, there are several options. The Maglev Train, a magnetic levitation train, is the fastest way to get to the city center, whisking you from the airport to the Longyang Road Metro Station in just about 8 minutes. The cost is reasonable, about ¥50 ($7 USD) one-way, and it runs frequently throughout the day. Alternatively, taxis and airport buses are readily available, though the taxi ride will take about 30 minutes, depending on traffic.

If you're flying domestically into Shanghai, you'll likely land at Shanghai Hongqiao International Airport (SHA), which is the main airport for flights within China. Located about 13 kilometers (8 miles) from the city center, Hongqiao is smaller and less hectic than Pudong, but still very efficient and well-equipped. It's the preferred choice for travelers coming from other parts of China, as it handles the majority of domestic flights. If you're coming in from another major Chinese city like Beijing, Guangzhou, or Chengdu, there are frequent, short flights available on airlines such as China Eastern Airlines, Air China, and Hainan Airlines. These flights are often quite affordable, with prices typically ranging from ¥300 to ¥1,000 (roughly $40 to $140 USD), depending on the route and time of booking.

Booking domestic flights within China is very straightforward. You can book through online travel platforms like Ctrip (Trip.com), or directly through the airline's website. Ctrip is particularly popular among locals and international travelers, as it offers great discounts, customer service in English, and the ability to easily book trains, flights, and accommodations. Many domestic flights within China are quite affordable, especially if you book well in advance, but it's important to note that prices can rise during peak travel times such as the Chinese New Year (Spring Festival) or Golden Week holidays.

For those who prefer not to fly, or for travelers already within China, Shanghai is also extremely well-connected by high-speed trains. High-speed rail in China has seen a massive expansion in recent years, making it an efficient and comfortable way to travel between cities. Shanghai's two main train stations, Shanghai Hongqiao Railway Station and Shanghai Railway Station, serve as the starting points for many high-speed trains traveling to and from other major cities like Beijing, Hangzhou, Nanjing, and even Guangzhou. These trains are incredibly fast, with some routes reaching speeds of over 200 mph (320 km/h), and they offer a comfortable, stress-free alternative to flying.

Booking high-speed train tickets can be done through multiple online platforms, such as 12306, China's official railway website, or third-party platforms like Ctrip or Travel China Guide. Tickets for high-speed trains can be relatively affordable, with a one-way journey between Beijing and Shanghai, for example, costing between ¥500 to ¥1,000 (around $70 to $140 USD) for standard class, depending on the time of booking and availability. For first-class tickets, you can expect to pay a bit more, but the extra space and comfort may be worth it for a longer journey.

One of the great things about China's high-speed rail system is the convenience and accessibility it offers. The trains are punctual and comfortable, with clean, spacious seating, Wi-Fi, and refreshments available for purchase. If you're traveling within Shanghai itself, you can take the metro to the train stations, making it incredibly easy to hop on a train without worrying about complicated transfers or getting lost. Plus, the train stations are modern and well-equipped with clear signage in both Chinese and English, so navigating the system is relatively simple.

When planning your trip, it's helpful to think about which option best fits your schedule, comfort preferences, and budget. While flights into Shanghai can be the fastest option, high-speed trains offer a more scenic and relaxed journey, especially for those traveling between other Chinese cities. Regardless of your choice, Shanghai's transportation infrastructure ensures that getting to the city is a smooth and straightforward experience.

Whether you're flying in from abroad or taking a domestic flight or high-speed train, the journey to Shanghai is just the beginning of an unforgettable adventure. From the moment you step off the plane or train and into the heart of this bustling city, you'll find yourself surrounded by a blend of modernity and tradition, where the old and new coexist in a dazzling display of culture, food, and sights.

Now that you know how to get to Shanghai, it's time to start looking forward to all the incredible experiences awaiting you. The city's unique blend of East and West, its mesmerizing skyline, and its rich cultural heritage are all waiting for you to explore. From the famous Bund to the eclectic neighborhoods, there's so much to see and do. So pack your bags, book your flight or train ticket, and get ready for an unforgettable adventure in one of the world's most exciting cities.

Visa Requirements and Entry Formalities

If you're planning a short visit to Shanghai, the 144-Hour Visa-Free Transit Policy might just be your ticket in. This policy is available to travelers from a number of countries, including the United States, the United Kingdom, Canada, Australia, and most EU member states. If you qualify, you can stay in Shanghai (and other cities in the Yangtze River Delta region) for up to 144 hours, or six days, without needing to apply for a visa. It's an excellent option for those who are just passing through Shanghai on their way to another destination, or for those who want to explore the city during a brief layover.

To take advantage of this policy, you'll need to meet certain criteria. First, you must be traveling on an international flight to and from China, with Shanghai as your port of entry. You'll also need to provide proof of onward travel to a third country or region within 144 hours of your arrival. This means that your next destination must be a non-Chinese city, and you should have a valid ticket for that journey. For example, if you're flying from New York to Shanghai and then continuing to Tokyo, the 144-hour policy would apply, and you wouldn't need to apply for a visa. However, if you're traveling on a domestic flight or without an onward ticket, you won't be eligible for the 144-hour visa-free transit.

The process to benefit from this policy is quite simple. Upon arriving at Shanghai Pudong International Airport (PVG), you'll head to the designated 144-Hour Visa-Free Transit counter at immigration. The staff will verify your eligibility based on your passport, flight ticket, and other documents. Once your eligibility is confirmed, you'll receive a special visa-free transit stamp that will allow you to enter Shanghai and stay for up to 144 hours. It's important to note that during this time, you are allowed to travel within Shanghai and the surrounding areas, but you cannot travel to other parts of China.

For travelers who do not qualify for the visa-free transit or who plan to stay longer than 144 hours, the standard tourist visa (L Visa) is the most common option. The process of applying for a tourist visa to China is relatively straightforward but requires some preparation. The first step is to gather all the necessary documents, which are outlined by the Chinese consulate or embassy in your country. You'll need a valid passport with at least six months of validity remaining and two blank visa pages, a completed visa application form (which can usually be downloaded from the Chinese consulate's website), a recent passport-sized photo, and proof of travel arrangements, including your flight ticket and hotel reservation in Shanghai.

One of the most critical steps in the process is providing proof of your accommodation in Shanghai. The Chinese authorities want to ensure that you have a place to stay for the duration of your trip, so be sure to have a hotel reservation or an invitation letter from a friend or family member if you're staying with someone in

Shanghai. If you're unsure about where to stay, I recommend booking a hotel in advance through reputable websites like Booking.com or Airbnb, which will allow you to provide the necessary confirmation details for your visa application. Additionally, you might be asked to provide proof of sufficient funds to cover your stay in Shanghai, which could include bank statements, credit card statements, or a letter from your employer.

The next step is to submit your application to the Chinese consulate or embassy in your home country. In most cases, you'll need to visit the consulate in person, but there are also services available that allow you to submit your application by mail. The processing time for a tourist visa is typically around 4-5 business days, though it may take longer if additional documents are requested or if you're applying during a peak travel season. You can choose to expedite the process for an additional fee, which can be particularly helpful if you're traveling on short notice. The cost of the tourist visa can vary depending on your nationality, but on average, it ranges from $140 to $200 USD for a single-entry visa. For citizens of some countries, such as the United States, the fee may be higher, and multiple-entry visas can cost even more.

Once your visa is approved, you'll receive a sticker in your passport that allows you to enter China. The length of stay granted with a tourist visa typically ranges from 30 to 60 days, though this can vary based on the consulate's discretion. Upon arrival in Shanghai, you'll need to go through immigration, where the immigration officer will verify your visa and entry information. It's worth noting that, while the tourist visa is relatively simple to obtain, you'll need to adhere to the conditions of your visa during your stay in Shanghai. Overstaying your visa can lead to fines, deportation, or being banned from reentering China, so be sure to keep track of your entry and exit dates.

If you're planning to extend your stay in Shanghai beyond the duration allowed by your tourist visa, you may be able to apply for an extension through the local Exit-Entry Administration Bureau in Shanghai. Extensions are typically granted for an additional 30 days, but there's no guarantee, and the application process can be time-consuming. If you plan to stay for an extended period, it's worth researching this process in advance, but it's always better to plan for a shorter stay and then apply for an extension if necessary.

One more thing to keep in mind is that China has strict regulations regarding visas and immigration, and Shanghai is no exception. Customs officers may ask you to provide additional documentation upon arrival, such as a return flight ticket or proof of sufficient funds. It's always a good idea to carry extra copies of your documents, just in case you're asked for them. If you're unsure about any part of the process or have questions about your eligibility for a visa or the 144-hour visa-free transit, don't hesitate to contact your local Chinese consulate or embassy for clarification. They can provide you with the most up-to-date information and guidance for your specific situation.

Navigating visa requirements and entry formalities for Shanghai can seem a bit daunting at first, but with a bit of preparation, it's a smooth and straightforward process. Whether you're taking advantage of the 144-hour visa-free transit or applying for a tourist visa, knowing what to expect can make your journey to Shanghai much more enjoyable. Once you've passed through immigration and stepped foot in this vibrant, fast-paced city, all the efforts of planning your visa will feel well worth it as you embark on your adventure through one of China's most exciting destinations.

Budgeting Your Trip

First, let's talk about accommodation, which is one of the major expenses for most travelers. In Shanghai, the range of options is vast, catering to every budget imaginable. If you're looking to save a bit of money, you'll be pleased to know that there are a number of affordable hostels and guesthouses scattered throughout the city, especially near the major tourist spots. A bed in a dormitory-style room in a decent hostel will generally cost you between ¥100 to ¥200 ($13 to $26 USD) per night. For a private room, you're looking at around ¥250 to ¥400 ($32 to $52 USD) per night, depending on the location and time of year. These places are often clean, comfortable, and conveniently located near metro stations, making them ideal for budget-conscious travelers.

If you're aiming for a more comfortable experience or prefer a bit more privacy, budget hotels or mid-range chains are also plentiful in Shanghai. Many of these hotels offer great value for money, with prices ranging from ¥400 to ¥800 ($52 to $105 USD) per night. These hotels generally provide free Wi-Fi, breakfast, and basic amenities, ensuring that you have everything you need for a pleasant stay without spending too much. Areas like Jing'an, Xintiandi, and the French Concession are popular spots for both budget and mid-range accommodations, with easy access to local attractions.

Of course, if you're looking for a luxurious experience, Shanghai offers some of the best high-end hotels in Asia. Prices for these upscale accommodations can range from ¥1,000 to ¥3,000 ($130 to $400 USD) per night, with even higher rates for five-star hotels located along the Bund, which offer stunning views of the city's skyline. While these places are certainly extravagant, they provide an unforgettable experience for those willing to splurge a little. Think world-class amenities, rooftop bars with sweeping city views, and impeccable service.

When it comes to food, Shanghai is a food lover's paradise. The city is famous for its delicious street food, mouthwatering dumplings, and local delicacies like xiaolongbao (soup dumplings) and shengjianbao (pan-fried dumplings). For budget travelers, street food is a great option, and you'll find plenty of stalls selling tasty treats at very affordable prices. A quick bite like a baozi (steamed bun) or a skewer of grilled meat will cost you just ¥10 to ¥30 ($1.30 to $4 USD). If you're in the mood for

something more filling, a bowl of noodles or fried rice from a local eatery will usually set you back about ¥30 to ¥60 ($4 to $8 USD).

If you're craving something a bit more substantial, there are numerous inexpensive restaurants throughout Shanghai serving up delicious Chinese cuisine. For a hearty meal at a mid-range restaurant, expect to pay around ¥80 to ¥150 ($10 to $20 USD) per person. Restaurants that specialize in regional Chinese dishes—such as Sichuan, Cantonese, or Jiangsu cuisine—are a great way to explore the diverse flavors of the country without spending too much. Many of these places offer family-style dining, where you can share a variety of dishes with friends or fellow travelers, making it a fun and affordable way to enjoy a meal.

For those who prefer international cuisine or fine dining, Shanghai has a wide selection of restaurants offering everything from sushi to Italian pasta. A meal at a more upscale restaurant will typically cost between ¥200 to ¥500 ($26 to $65 USD) per person, depending on the restaurant's style and location. Dining at luxury restaurants, especially those with views of the Bund or rooftop bars, can run significantly higher, but the experience often includes not just food but an unforgettable atmosphere.

Now, let's talk about activities. Shanghai is a city with so much to offer, from historical landmarks and cultural experiences to modern entertainment and shopping. If you're interested in sightseeing, there are several must-see attractions that won't cost you a fortune. Visiting the Bund, Shanghai's iconic waterfront promenade, is free, and it's one of the best places to get a feel for the city's stunning skyline. You can also take a stroll along Nanjing Road, China's busiest shopping street, where window shopping doesn't cost a thing. Other must-visit spots like the Jade Buddha Temple and the Shanghai Museum have very reasonable entry fees, usually ranging from ¥20 to ¥50 ($3 to $7 USD). If you're into modern art, the Shanghai Museum of Contemporary Art and the Power Station of Art are great places to explore, with admission often under ¥50 ($7 USD).

For those who enjoy parks and green spaces, a visit to Yuyuan Garden, a beautiful classical Chinese garden in the heart of the city, will cost you around ¥40 ($5 USD) for entry. On the other hand, if you want to experience the dizzying heights of Shanghai, a ticket to the Shanghai Tower's observation deck will cost you around ¥180 ($23 USD), but the panoramic views of the city are well worth it. The price of activities like river cruises on the Huangpu River can range from ¥50 to ¥200 ($6 to $26 USD), depending on the type of cruise, so there's something for every budget.

One of the best things about Shanghai is that it's a city that caters to all types of travelers. If you're looking to save money, you can easily get by on a daily budget of ¥200 to ¥400 ($26 to $52 USD) by sticking to budget accommodations, eating street food, and enjoying the city's many free or low-cost attractions. If you're more interested in indulging in some luxury, you'll find plenty of options for pampering yourself with fine dining, upscale hotels, and exclusive experiences, but even in those cases, Shanghai still offers value for the experience. For a comfortable trip with a balance of dining out, staying in mid-range hotels, and enjoying a few paid attractions, you might expect to spend anywhere from ¥500 to ¥1,000 ($65 to $130 USD) per day.

To stretch your travel budget even further, consider using Shanghai's well-developed public transportation system. The metro is incredibly efficient, with fares ranging from ¥3 to ¥9 ($0.40 to $1.20 USD) per ride, making it an affordable way to get around. Taxis are also relatively inexpensive, but they can add up if you're traveling long distances, so it's a good idea to rely on public transport whenever possible.

Packing for Shanghai

Shanghai's weather can be tricky to predict, so it's important to plan ahead based on the season you're visiting. The city experiences four distinct seasons, each with its own unique climate, and packing the right clothing will ensure that you stay comfortable while exploring.

If you're visiting during the summer months, from June to August, you'll want to pack light, breathable clothing. Shanghai can get hot and humid, with temperatures frequently reaching into the 90s (around 32–35°C), so lightweight cottons and linens are your best friends. Pack short-sleeve shirts, tank tops, and breathable dresses that will keep you cool as you wander through the city. If you're planning on spending any time in the city's many parks or walking along the Huangpu River, bring along a good pair of comfortable sneakers or walking shoes. In summer, you'll definitely want to wear sun protection – a hat, sunglasses, and high-SPF sunscreen are essentials. Be sure to bring a light, foldable umbrella too, as summer in Shanghai can also mean sudden downpours.

The fall season, from September to November, is one of the best times to visit Shanghai. The weather is cooler and much more pleasant, with temperatures ranging from 15°C to 25°C (59°F to 77°F). It's still mild enough to enjoy the outdoor sights, but you might feel a slight chill in the evenings. This is when you can get away with packing a versatile wardrobe. Layering is key. A few stylish, lightweight sweaters, long-sleeve shirts, and a light jacket should cover you for the majority of the day. You may also want to pack a pair of comfortable jeans or chinos, as Shanghai is known for its fashion-forward locals, and you'll feel right at home blending in with the trendy crowd. Comfortable yet stylish shoes are a must, as you'll likely do a lot of walking around the city, from sightseeing in Old Shanghai to exploring the elegant French Concession area. It's worth noting that while the city looks beautiful in the fall with its autumn leaves, it can also be a bit rainy, so be prepared with a compact umbrella or a waterproof jacket.

Winter in Shanghai (December to February) can be surprisingly cold, especially given the city's humid subtropical climate. While the temperatures rarely dip below freezing, it can feel damp and chilly, especially with the constant breeze coming from the river. The average temperature in January hovers around 5°C to 8°C (41°F to 46°F), but with the wind chill, it can feel much colder. For this, you'll need to pack warmer clothing. A medium-weight coat or insulated jacket will be necessary, and layering is again the best way to keep warm. Thermal shirts or sweaters, scarves, gloves, and a hat are key essentials for comfort. If you're planning to take public transportation or walk around for extended periods, a pair of waterproof, insulated shoes or boots will protect your feet from the dampness and cold. It's also worth noting that central heating isn't

ubiquitous in public spaces, so some areas like shopping malls or restaurants can feel cold indoors too. Therefore, dressing in layers that you can easily add or remove is important for maintaining comfort throughout the day.

Spring, from March to May, is another fantastic time to visit Shanghai. The temperatures are mild and gradually warm up, making it perfect for exploring the city at a relaxed pace. During this season, temperatures range from 10°C to 20°C (50°F to 68°F), so packing layers is once again a smart idea. A medium-weight jacket or trench coat will serve you well in the cooler mornings, while lighter clothing is fine for the warmer afternoons. Spring is also the season for cherry blossoms and blooming flowers, so you might want to pack a camera or smartphone to capture the beauty of Shanghai's parks and gardens. Comfortable sneakers are still a must for walking, as you'll want to explore outdoor sights like Yuyuan Garden or the Longhua Temple, which are particularly beautiful in spring. Be sure to also bring a scarf or shawl to layer over your outfit in the evenings, as the weather can still be a bit unpredictable.

No matter when you visit Shanghai, there are some items you'll want to pack regardless of the season. First and foremost, don't forget your power adapter! Shanghai uses the standard Chinese plug type, which is different from most Western countries, so bringing a universal adapter is essential to keep your devices charged as you explore. Another important item to pack is a reusable water bottle, as staying hydrated is key in a bustling city like Shanghai. The tap water is not potable, but you can buy bottled water easily, or if you're eco-conscious, fill your water bottle up at cafes or restaurants. Also, you'll want to make sure you have a good camera or smartphone for all the incredible sights, from the soaring skyline at the Lujiazui district to the more tranquil, traditional scenes found in the old neighborhoods of Shanghai. A portable charger can come in handy if you plan on taking lots of photos and need to juice up on the go.

When it comes to toiletries and personal care items, Shanghai has no shortage of stores selling everything you might need, but it's still worth packing your preferred items, especially if you have specific brands or products you rely on. For example, you may want to pack travel-size versions of shampoo, conditioner, soap, and any skincare essentials, as these can be more expensive and harder to find in the small sizes you're used to. Additionally, pack any medication or health-related items you might need during your trip, as pharmacies in China may not carry the exact same brands or types of over-the-counter medicine that you're accustomed to.

Health and Safety Tips

One of the first things you'll notice when you arrive in Shanghai is the sheer number of people. The city's population is over 24 million, making it one of the most densely populated cities in the world. The streets are filled with locals, tourists, and commuters, especially around popular areas like Nanjing Road and the Bund. While Shanghai is generally very safe, these crowded areas can pose a few challenges, particularly when it comes to pickpocketing or losing your bearings in the midst of all the people.

It's important to stay aware of your surroundings, especially when you're in busy spots like subway stations, markets, or shopping malls. For starters, keep your valuables close to you. A cross-body bag or a money belt is a great choice for keeping your phone, wallet, and passport secure. It's also wise to avoid walking around with too much cash. Instead, use mobile payment apps like Alipay or WeChat Pay, which are widely accepted and incredibly convenient. In fact,

Shanghai has an incredibly advanced cashless payment system, and many small vendors, cafes, and even street food stalls will prefer this method.

When navigating the crowds, you'll want to be cautious of traffic, particularly the ever-bustling roads where motorbikes, cars, and buses zoom by at high speeds. Shanghai is known for its impressive public transport system, but the streets can sometimes feel like controlled chaos. Pedestrian crossings are often overlooked, so make sure to stay alert when crossing streets, even at designated crossings. The metro system, although efficient and affordable, can also get extremely packed, particularly during rush hours. If you're planning to travel by subway, try to avoid peak hours (roughly 7:30-9:30 AM and 5:30-7:30 PM), when trains are at their fullest. Don't be surprised if people jostle you to get in or out of trains, as personal space is often at a premium during these times.

In the face of all this, staying healthy in Shanghai isn't too difficult, but like any big city, there are a few health considerations to be aware of. The air quality in Shanghai can sometimes be less than ideal, particularly during the colder months, when smog can accumulate. While it's not always a problem, you may find that your respiratory system feels a little under the weather if you're sensitive to pollution. If you're not used to air pollution, consider wearing a mask, particularly if you're spending a lot of time outdoors or in crowded areas. Many people in Shanghai wear masks for health reasons, especially in areas with high pollution levels, and it's a common practice. If you do suffer from asthma or respiratory conditions, it's a good idea to keep any necessary medication with you at all times, just in case. A quick note on weather-related health concerns: Shanghai can get quite humid during the summer months, with temperatures soaring above 30°C (86°F). If you're visiting during this time, make sure to stay hydrated, wear sunscreen, and protect yourself from the sun with hats and sunglasses.

Now, let's talk about healthcare and emergency services. While most visitors to Shanghai will not encounter serious health problems, it's important to know where to go if something does happen. The city has a number of modern hospitals and clinics, with many of them catering specifically to expatriates. International hospitals, such as the United Family Healthcare and Shanghai United Family Hospital, provide high-quality care and have English-speaking staff. They offer a range of services, from basic checkups to more serious medical treatments. If you need non-emergency care, you can always visit a local pharmacy. There are pharmacies located throughout the city, and the staff in most of them can assist with over-the-counter medications for minor ailments like colds, headaches, or digestive issues. In the event of an emergency, you can dial 120 for an ambulance, but keep in mind that response times may vary, particularly in more crowded or outlying areas of the city.

If you're ever unsure about where to go for medical treatment, don't hesitate to ask your hotel's front desk for assistance or guidance. Many hotels in Shanghai, especially those catering to international tourists, have partnerships with hospitals or can connect you with English-speaking medical professionals. Additionally, if you have travel insurance, it's a good idea to check ahead of time whether it covers medical treatment abroad and if there are any preferred hospitals or doctors you should visit.

As you explore the city, you'll likely come across many parks, green spaces, and local hospitals that are well-maintained and accessible for those who may need assistance. Shanghai is a city that puts great emphasis on modern infrastructure, so finding medical help or assistance in any other emergency is straightforward, even for those who don't speak Mandarin. Most larger hotels will have staff who are fluent in English, and they can assist in emergency situations. It's also important to have the contact details of your country's embassy or consulate in Shanghai just in case you need urgent help.

Another point to consider when traveling in Shanghai is the local food scene. The city is known for its incredible variety of food, from the delicious soup dumplings of Xiaolongbao to street-side snacks like baozi and skewered meats. While food is generally safe to eat in Shanghai, it's always a good idea to be cautious if you have a sensitive stomach or if you're not used to spicy or greasy food. Stick to busy restaurants and street food stalls that look clean and well-maintained, as these tend to be the safest options. Avoid drinking tap water, as it is not considered safe for tourists. Instead, opt for bottled water, which is easy to find at almost every corner store.

If you do find yourself experiencing any food-related discomfort, there are plenty of pharmacies in Shanghai where you can find remedies for indigestion, upset stomachs, or mild food poisoning. Many pharmacies carry basic over-the-counter medications, and if necessary, they can help you find what you need to feel better.

MUST-SEE ATTRACTIONS AND LANDMARKS

Historic Landmarks

The Bund, with its iconic waterfront promenade, is perhaps Shanghai's most recognizable landmark. This stretch along the Huangpu River is a fascinating showcase of the city's history, where colonial-era architecture meets modern Shanghai in a dramatic visual contrast. The Bund is located in the heart of Shanghai's historic district, along Zhongshan East Road, and offers one of the most stunning views of the city's skyline. The area is home to 52 historical buildings, each a reminder of the city's role as a hub of international trade during the early 20th century. These buildings, built in a blend of European architectural styles—neo-classical, gothic, and art deco—were once the headquarters of major banks, shipping companies, and consulates. Walking along the Bund feels like taking a step back in time.

You can explore the old customs house, the Bank of China building, and the Shanghai Club building, each brimming with a colonial charm that tells the story of Shanghai's early growth as a major trading port. The best time to visit the Bund is either early in the morning, when the air is crisp and the crowds are thin, or at night, when the city's lights create a magical atmosphere. At night, the skyline across the river, particularly the futuristic Oriental Pearl Tower and the towering skyscrapers of Pudong, glitter like a sea of diamonds. It's the perfect time to take photos and marvel at the contrast between Shanghai's colonial past and its futuristic present. The

Bund is easily accessible from the East Nanjing Road Metro Station or by taking a ferry across the river from the Pudong side. Whether you're admiring the view from the promenade or taking a boat ride on the river, the Bund offers a unique opportunity to connect with both Shanghai's past and its present.

Not too far from the Bund is *Yuyuan Garden,* a serene and historically significant oasis of calm in the heart of the city. Located at 218 Anren Street in the old city of Shanghai, this classical Chinese garden dates back to the Ming Dynasty, over 400 years ago, and remains a stunning example of traditional Chinese landscaping and design. The garden was originally built by Pan Yunduan, a wealthy government official, as a private retreat for his parents. It was later expanded into the vast and intricate garden that visitors see today. When you step into Yuyuan Garden, you're stepping into a world of intricate rockeries, winding paths, koi-filled ponds, pavilions, and ancient trees.

The garden is designed in the traditional Suzhou style, with each section offering a different aesthetic experience. The "Great Rockery," an artificial mountain made from jagged rocks, is the focal point of the garden and offers visitors a chance to climb up and look out over the peaceful surroundings. The winding paths lead to hidden courtyards, where you can find beautiful wooden carvings, delicate bridges, and stone lanterns that date back centuries. Yuyuan Garden is not only a place of beauty but a reflection of the cultural and artistic ideals of the Ming Dynasty. It offers a rare glimpse into the sophisticated aesthetic of the time, with its intricate design and meticulous attention to detail.

When visiting Yuyuan, be sure to stop by the nearby Yuyuan Bazaar. This bustling market offers traditional Chinese goods, including tea, silk, jade, and handcrafted souvenirs. It's a great place to explore after taking in the garden's tranquility. The best time to visit Yuyuan Garden is in the early morning or late afternoon when the garden is less crowded. The hours of operation are generally from 8:30 AM to 5:30 PM, but it's advisable to check in advance as opening times can vary during peak tourist seasons or special events. The garden can be reached easily from the Yuyuan Garden Metro Station, and while the entry fee is modest, it's well worth the cost for the experience of walking through history.

Another essential stop on your journey through Shanghai's historic landmarks is the *Jade Buddha Temple.* Located at 170 Anyuan Road, in the Zhabei District, the Jade Buddha Temple is a peaceful haven that offers both spiritual solace and a window into the rich cultural history of Buddhism in Shanghai. Founded in 1882, the temple is one of the city's most revered places of worship, drawing visitors from around the world who come to admire its stunning architecture, the serene atmosphere, and the beautiful jade Buddha statues that the temple is named for. The main attraction at the Jade Buddha Temple is undoubtedly the two jade Buddha statues: the sitting Buddha and the reclining Buddha.

The statues, which are carved from a single block of Burmese jade, are simply breathtaking in their serene beauty and intricate craftsmanship. The sitting Buddha, in particular, is awe-inspiring, measuring over 1.9 meters tall and weighing over 3 tons. The reclining Buddha, representing the Buddha's final moments, is equally impressive in size

and craftsmanship. The temple itself is a classic example of traditional Chinese Buddhist architecture, with elegant wooden beams, gold-painted decorations, and an air of tranquility that makes it easy to lose track of time. The temple is also home to several smaller halls, each dedicated to a different Buddhist deity, and these areas are often less crowded, making it a great spot for meditation or reflection.

One of the temple's highlights is the serene atmosphere, which makes it a peaceful escape from the bustling city outside. Visitors can sit in the temple's courtyard, take in the calm surroundings, or even participate in the temple's offerings and prayers, a wonderful opportunity to connect with the local culture. The Jade Buddha Temple is open daily from 8:00 AM to 4:30 PM, and while there is a small admission fee, it's a place worth visiting for its quiet beauty and spiritual significance. It's also located just a short walk from the Shanghai Railway Station, making it easy to get to from most parts of the city.

Modern Marvels

Among the most impressive modern marvels in Shanghai, three landmarks stand out in their sheer scale, beauty, and the experiences they offer. The Shanghai Tower, the *Oriental Pearl TV Tower,* and the ever-vibrant Nanjing Road embody the city's forward-thinking spirit and its deep-rooted connection to both tradition and innovation.

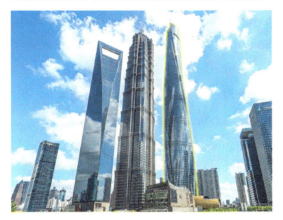

The **Shanghai Tower** is nothing short of breathtaking. Standing at 632 meters, this glass and steel behemoth is not only the tallest building in Shanghai, but also the tallest skyscraper in all of China. Located in the heart of the Lujiazui Finance and Trade Zone, in the Pudong district, the Shanghai Tower is part of the city's skyline-defining trio, alongside the Jin Mao Tower and the World Financial Center. It's hard to miss the Shanghai Tower, with its unique spiral design, which tapers as it rises, creating a sense of fluid motion that mimics the traditional Chinese symbol for water. This architectural feat is a testament to Shanghai's rapid development and commitment to blending cutting-edge design with sustainability.

But it's not just the structure itself that impresses; the views from the top are truly a sight to behold. If you visit the observation deck on the 118th floor, you'll be treated to an unparalleled panoramic view of Shanghai. On a clear day, you can gaze out over the entire city, from the winding Huangpu River to the sprawling expanse of the city's skyline, dotted with towering skyscrapers that stretch into the distance. The Shanghai Tower is not just a tower; it's a statement of what Shanghai represents today—forward-thinking, innovative, and constantly evolving. The best time to visit the tower is in the late afternoon or at dusk, when the city begins to sparkle under the golden hour light and transitions into the evening's glow. The observation deck is open daily from 8:30 AM to 10:00 PM, though it's recommended to get tickets early to avoid long queues, especially during peak seasons. To reach the tower, simply take Line 2 on the Shanghai Metro to Lujiazui Station, which is just a short walk from the building.

Just a stone's throw from the Shanghai Tower, you'll find another one of the city's most iconic landmarks: the **Oriental Pearl TV Tower.** Rising 468 meters above the Huangpu River, this striking, space-age structure is one of Shanghai's most recognized symbols. Built in the 1990s, the Oriental Pearl Tower was, for many years, the tallest building in the city, and its unique design—comprising multiple spheres stacked on top of each other—makes it look like something straight out of a sci-fi movie. It's not just a visual marvel but an architectural triumph, and its neon-lit, glowing form has become a defining feature of Shanghai's skyline. When you visit the Oriental Pearl TV Tower, there's no shortage of things to do.

For starters, head up to the observation decks located in the lower spheres to get panoramic views of the city. The observation deck on the 263rd floor offers a breathtaking 360-degree view, while the "Glass Floor" on the 259th floor gives you the thrill of looking straight down to the ground below. It's an exhilarating experience that's not for the faint of heart, but if you're looking for an adrenaline rush, it's definitely worth a visit. You can also visit the revolving restaurant located in the top sphere for a truly unique dining experience, as it rotates 360 degrees while you enjoy your meal. The tower is open daily from 8:30 AM to 9:30 PM, and while tickets can be purchased at the entrance, it's advisable to buy them online in advance to avoid the long lines. To get there, the easiest way is to take Line 2 on the metro and alight at Lujiazui Station, which is only a few minutes' walk from the tower.

Another modern marvel that reflects Shanghai's dynamic energy is *Nanjing Road.* This iconic street is the heartbeat of the city's shopping scene and is often compared to Times Square in New York or the Champs-Élysées in Paris. Stretching for 5.5 kilometers from the Bund to the Jing'an Temple, Nanjing Road is lined with a dazzling array of shops, restaurants, malls, and historic buildings. The street is particularly famous for its neon lights, which illuminate the area well into the night, creating an almost surreal atmosphere that's a blend of modern consumerism and old-world charm. Whether you're looking to shop for the latest luxury goods or hunting for unique souvenirs, Nanjing Road has something for everyone.

The pedestrian section, which starts near People's Square, is a shopper's paradise, filled with department stores, international boutiques, and brand-name shops. If you're in the mood for high-end shopping, you'll find flagship stores for brands like Louis Vuitton, Gucci, and Prada, all housed in stunning glass-and-steel buildings that reflect the city's rapidly changing skyline. But Nanjing Road is not just about shopping. It's a place where history and modernity coexist. As you stroll along, take a moment to admire the colonial-era architecture that still lines the streets in between the modern shopping malls. For a taste of local culture, pop into one of the many traditional teahouses or eateries that dot the area. One of the highlights of Nanjing Road is its vibrant street food scene.

While you're here, be sure to sample some of Shanghai's famous snacks, like xiaolongbao (steamed dumplings), shengjianbao (pan-fried dumplings), and tanghulu (candied fruit on sticks). The best time to visit Nanjing Road is in the evening when the neon lights create an electric atmosphere. The street is open 24/7, but the busiest and most lively times are typically after 5:00 PM, when the shopping crowd peaks. Getting to Nanjing Road is easy: simply hop on Line 2 or Line 1 of the Shanghai Metro and get off at People's Square Station, which is conveniently located right at the beginning of the pedestrian shopping area.

Cultural Highlights

Your cultural journey in Shanghai begins at the *Shanghai Museum*, an architectural marvel located in the heart of People's Square. The museum itself is a stunning piece of modern design, with a cylindrical structure surrounded by a large, open courtyard. Inside, it houses one of the most impressive collections of Chinese art and artifacts in the world, spanning over 5,000 years of history. As you step through the museum's grand doors, you are immediately greeted by a sense of awe, not only from the scale of the exhibits but from the sheer wealth of history encapsulated in its walls.

The museum's collection is divided into 11 main galleries, each dedicated to a specific type of art or artifact. One of the most captivating displays is the ancient bronzes section, which showcases intricately crafted vessels from the Shang and Zhou dynasties, reflecting China's early achievements in metallurgy. The ceramics collection is equally impressive, with beautiful porcelain pieces from the Tang and Song dynasties, each telling a story of artistic evolution and cultural importance. If you're someone who appreciates fine art, the museum's calligraphy and painting collections will also leave you spellbound, with works dating back to the Tang Dynasty.

The museum is not just a passive experience; it's a place where you can immerse yourself in the stories behind the artifacts, thanks to well-curated exhibits and informative displays. The best time to visit the Shanghai Museum is in the early morning or late afternoon, as it tends to be busiest in the middle of the day, especially during weekends and public holidays. The museum is open from 9 AM to 5 PM, and entry is free, which is a real treat considering the wealth of art it offers. To get there, simply take Line 1, Line 2, or Line 8 of the Shanghai Metro and alight at People's Square Station, which is just a short walk from the museum.

Next on your cultural exploration is the *Longhua Temple and Pagoda,* a tranquil retreat nestled amidst the hustle and bustle of the city. Located in the southwestern part of Shanghai, the Longhua Temple is the oldest and largest temple complex in the city, dating back to the Three Kingdoms period (220–280 AD). Stepping into Longhua Temple feels like entering another world. The air is filled with the fragrant scent of incense, and the sound of chanting monks adds to the serene atmosphere. The temple is dedicated to the Buddha and is one of the most significant Buddhist temples in Shanghai.

The Longhua Pagoda, standing at an impressive 40 meters tall, is one of the main attractions of the temple complex. Originally built in the 3rd century, the pagoda has been rebuilt several times, with the current structure dating back to the 10th century. Visitors can climb the pagoda's nine stories, offering a panoramic view of the temple grounds and the surrounding area. The architecture of Longhua Temple is a beautiful example of ancient Chinese design, with sweeping eaves, intricate wooden carvings, and golden statues of Buddha that create an atmosphere of reverence. Apart from the pagoda, another must-see is the Hall of the Heavenly Kings, which houses massive, colorful statues of four guardian kings.

The temple is also home to peaceful courtyards, where you can sit and meditate or simply enjoy the peaceful surroundings. Longhua Temple is a popular destination for both locals and tourists, especially around Chinese New Year, when many come to pray for good fortune. To visit the temple, take Line 11 of the Shanghai Metro and alight at Longhua Station. From there, it's just a short walk to the temple entrance. It's best to visit the temple in the morning when the crowds are lighter, and you can fully appreciate the peacefulness of the site. The temple is open daily from 7 AM to 5:30 PM, with a small entry fee of about 10 RMB.

No trip to Shanghai would be complete without a visit to the *Former French Concession,* a charming neighborhood that transports you back in time to the early 20th century. The French Concession, once a colonial district, is an area rich in history, with tree-lined streets, elegant European-style villas, and hidden cafés that offer a quiet respite from the city's fast pace. As you wander through the narrow lanes of the Former French Concession, you can't help but feel as though you're walking through a different era.

The architecture is distinctly European, with French-style townhouses, art-deco buildings, and ornate balconies that stand in stark contrast to the modern high-rises elsewhere in Shanghai. This area is perfect for a leisurely walk, where you can discover quirky boutiques, vintage shops, and local galleries. It's also home to some fantastic dining spots, from casual cafés to fine-dining restaurants, making it an ideal place for lunch or dinner. One of the highlights of the Former French Concession is the picturesque Fuxing Park, which was once a private garden for French expatriates. Today, it's a public park where locals practice tai chi, play mahjong, or simply enjoy a peaceful moment. Another must-see is the area around Wukang Road, often referred to as Shanghai's "most beautiful street," which is lined with charming old buildings and a relaxed, cosmopolitan vibe.

The Former French Concession is especially beautiful during the spring and autumn months when the trees lining the streets are in full bloom or adorned with golden leaves. It's also a great place to enjoy Shanghai's café culture, with numerous spots serving up delicious coffee and pastries. To reach the Former French Concession, take Line 1, Line 10, or Line 12 on the Shanghai

Metro, and get off at either Xujiahui Station or South Shaanxi Road Station. From there, it's just a short walk to explore the winding streets of this historic district. The best time to visit is in the early morning or late afternoon when the light is soft and the area feels more relaxed. While there's no official entrance fee to the Former French Concession, many of the cafes, shops, and galleries will invite you to linger and experience the local culture at your own pace.

These three cultural highlights in Shanghai provide a fascinating insight into the city's diverse heritage. From the ancient artifacts and artistic treasures of the Shanghai Museum to the spiritual tranquility of Longhua Temple, and the colonial charm of the Former French Concession, each destination offers something unique and unforgettable. Visiting these sites is not just about admiring architecture or artifacts; it's about connecting with the spirit of Shanghai

Natural Escapes

Your journey into nature begins at *Century Park*, a sprawling, lush expanse that covers 140 hectares of land in the heart of the Pudong New Area. If you're looking to escape the noise and crowds of the city, Century Park offers the perfect setting to unwind. It is the largest park in Shanghai, designed as a green oasis where locals and tourists alike can relax,

stroll, or enjoy a wide variety of outdoor activities. The park, which was opened in 2000, has been carefully crafted to balance natural beauty with human design, featuring a mix of open lawns, scenic lakes, flower gardens, and woodlands.

As you step into the park, you'll notice how the city seems to fade into the background, replaced by a sense of calm and freshness that's almost palpable. The park is beautifully landscaped, with winding paths that lead you through different thematic gardens. There's the classical Chinese Garden, where traditional Chinese landscaping elements like rockeries, ponds, and pavilions evoke the aesthetic of old-world gardens, and the European Garden, which has neat, manicured lawns and geometrical layouts. These distinct sections allow you to experience different styles of gardening from across the world, all within a single park.

For nature lovers, Century Park is more than just a space to walk and relax—it's a place to immerse yourself in the natural world. The park features a large lake where you can rent a boat and gently row across the water, taking in the surroundings at your own pace. Along the lake, you'll spot local birds, including migratory species that rest in the park during different seasons. It's also home to a diverse range of flora, with flower festivals in the spring and summer showcasing vibrant blooms like cherry blossoms, lotus flowers, and sunflowers. The park's green expanses are perfect for a leisurely picnic or simply lying on the grass, surrounded by the hum of nature.

If you enjoy a more active experience, Century Park offers a variety of recreational activities such as cycling, jogging, and even a large playground for families with children. Additionally, there are several cultural and art events hosted here throughout the year, from music festivals to outdoor exhibitions, adding an extra layer of vibrancy to the park. To get to Century Park, you can take Line 2 of the Shanghai Metro to Century Park Station, which is just a short walk from the park's main entrance. The park is open from 5 AM to 9 PM daily, and the entry fee is modest, usually around 10 RMB, though special events or certain areas may require a separate ticket. The best time to visit is during the early morning or late afternoon, when the air is cooler and the park feels especially peaceful.

Just a short distance away from the urban sprawl, another oasis awaits in the form of **_Binjiang Forest Park._** Nestled along the banks of the Huangpu River, Binjiang Forest Park is a quieter, more secluded park that offers stunning views of the river and the city's skyline. It's a natural haven, designed to offer a green escape with an emphasis on preserving the local environment. The park covers over 200 hectares and is a perfect blend of forested areas, wetlands, and river views. If you've spent your days exploring the hectic streets of downtown Shanghai, this park will feel like stepping into another world. The fresh river breeze, the gentle sounds of the water, and the rustling of leaves create a soothing atmosphere, inviting you to take a deep breath and slow down.

What sets Binjiang Forest Park apart from other green spaces in Shanghai is its connection to the Huangpu River. The park is carefully designed to integrate with the natural contours of the riverbank, with wide, grassy areas perfect for a peaceful walk along the water. The park's pathways are lined with trees, offering plenty of shaded spots where you can take a rest or simply enjoy the beauty of your surroundings. The views of the Huangpu River from here are spectacular, especially during sunset when the sky transforms into a vibrant canvas of reds, oranges, and pinks, reflecting off the water. This is an ideal spot for photographers or anyone looking to capture the beauty of Shanghai from a different perspective.

Binjiang Forest Park also offers a variety of outdoor activities, from cycling and running along the river paths to birdwatching in the park's wetlands. The park's ecosystem is rich with flora and fauna, and there's a chance you might spot a few of Shanghai's resident birds, including herons and egrets. For a more laid-back experience, you can find a peaceful spot along the riverbank to read a book or simply observe the boats drifting lazily by. If you enjoy spending time near water, there's also a small dock where you can rent a boat for a relaxing ride along the river, providing a serene view of both the natural surroundings and the city's iconic skyline. For those traveling with children, the park has several playgrounds and areas designed for family-friendly activities, ensuring that visitors of all ages can enjoy the space. The park is also home to several gardens, including a butterfly garden and a fragrant herb garden, offering even more opportunities to connect with nature.

To reach Binjiang Forest Park, you can take Line 7 of the Shanghai Metro and get off at Longcao Road Station. From there, it's a short bus ride or taxi ride to the park's entrance. The park is open daily from 5:30 AM to 6:30 PM, and there is a small entry fee of around 15 RMB. Like Century Park, the best times to visit are early in the morning or late in the afternoon, when the weather is cooler and the park is less crowded.

Nearby Day Trips

If you're looking for an enchanting escape that feels like stepping into a time capsule, then a visit to *Zhujiajiao Water Town* is an absolute must. Located just 45 minutes from downtown Shanghai by car or a little over an hour by public transportation, Zhujiajiao is an ancient water town known for its winding canals, traditional architecture, and charming stone bridges. Often referred to as the "Venice of Shanghai," this town is a place where time seems to slow down as you wander its cobblestone streets and cross its picturesque bridges. You'll find yourself captivated by the beauty of the traditional Ming and Qing dynasty-style buildings that line the waterways, many of which are now home to quaint tea houses, shops, and small eateries. The town's unique architecture and its canals—dating back over a thousand years—give Zhujiajiao a sense of being suspended in time.

One of the most delightful activities in Zhujiajiao is taking a boat ride along the canals. Whether you choose a traditional wooden boat or a small gondola-style boat, the serene journey along the water offers a chance to take in the stunning views of the town from a different angle. You'll pass by charming houses with their red lanterns, small bridges arching over the canals, and lush greenery that surrounds the water. It's not uncommon to see local residents going about their daily activities along the waterfront, adding a sense of authenticity to your visit. Apart from the boat rides, Zhujiajiao is also home to several interesting cultural landmarks. The Fangsheng Bridge, one of the town's

oldest and most famous landmarks, is a perfect spot for photos. Another highlight is the Zhujiajiao Ancient Town, which houses the elegant Kezhi Garden, a tranquil, traditional Chinese garden that will transport you into a world of classical beauty. The garden is adorned with ponds, pavilions, and serene walkways, offering a peaceful retreat for visitors seeking respite from the hustle and bustle of city life.

If you're craving more history and culture, Zhujiajiao is also home to a number of ancient temples, such as the Yuanjin Buddhist Temple and the Chenghuang Miao (Town God Temple), both of which provide insight into the spiritual traditions that have shaped the region for centuries. The best time to visit Zhujiajiao is during the spring or autumn months when the weather is mild and the town's beauty is in full bloom. However, visiting on weekdays is preferable as weekends tend to attract more crowds. To get there from Shanghai, you can take Metro Line 17 from the city center to Zhujiajiao Station, and then take a short bus or taxi ride to the town center. A visit to Zhujiajiao will give you a chance to experience the quieter side of China's rich cultural history, and it offers an unforgettable contrast to the speed and scale of Shanghai.

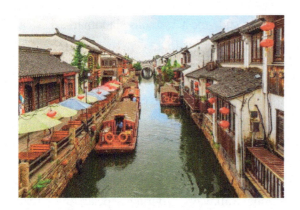

A short trip to *Suzhou*, just an hour away from Shanghai by high-speed train, is another fantastic way to spend a day immersed in China's ancient traditions. Known as the "Venice of the East," Suzhou is famous for its classical gardens, silk production, and picturesque waterways. The city has a long history dating back over 2,500 years, and it's often regarded as the cultural heart of Jiangsu Province. One of the must-see highlights in Suzhou is its stunning collection of classical Chinese gardens, which are recognized as UNESCO World Heritage Sites. These gardens are masterpieces of landscape design, where you'll find intricate stone carvings, elegant pavilions, serene ponds, and lush greenery. The Humble Administrator's Garden and the Lingering Garden are two of the most famous, both showcasing the perfect harmony between nature and human craftsmanship. A stroll through these gardens feels like stepping into a living work of art, with every step revealing a new perspective, a new beauty, or a hidden corner.

Beyond the gardens, Suzhou is renowned for its silk production, and a visit to one of the city's many silk factories offers an intriguing glimpse into this ancient industry. You can watch artisans at work, spinning delicate threads and creating beautiful silk textiles that have been prized for centuries. The Suzhou Silk Museum provides a deep dive into the city's silk heritage and history, explaining how Suzhou became the center of the silk trade during China's imperial dynasties. For those who enjoy a more hands-on experience, there are opportunities to purchase high-quality silk goods, from clothing to home decor, as a souvenir of your visit.

To reach Suzhou from Shanghai, simply take a high-speed train from Shanghai's Hongqiao Station, which will take you directly to Suzhou in around 25 minutes. Once in Suzhou, you'll find the city's famous gardens, such as the Lion Grove Garden and the Garden of the Master of Nets, within easy reach of the train station. Suzhou is also home to beautiful canals, and you can take a boat ride along the waterways to see the city from a different perspective. Suzhou's mild climate makes it an ideal destination year-round, though spring and autumn are particularly lovely for a leisurely walk through the gardens when the flowers are in bloom or the foliage is turning brilliant shades of red and gold.

A trip to Hangzhou, located about 2 hours by train or bus from Shanghai, offers a perfect way to escape the city and immerse yourself in nature's beauty. Known for the famous West Lake, Hangzhou is a city that embodies the traditional elegance and peaceful ambiance of ancient China. West Lake is the centerpiece of the city, and its poetic scenery has inspired poets, artists, and scholars for centuries. The lake is dotted with islands, pagodas, and temples, all surrounded by lush greenery and misty mountains in the distance. One of the best ways to experience the magic of West Lake is to take a leisurely boat ride, allowing you to glide across the calm waters while soaking in the natural beauty of the area. The views of the lake, especially during sunrise or sunset, are simply breathtaking.

Aside from West Lake, Hangzhou is also home to several ancient temples and pagodas, such as the Lingyin Temple, which is one of the largest and most famous Buddhist temples in China. The temple complex is tucked away in the mountains, surrounded by forested hills and dotted with ancient stone carvings, making it a serene and spiritual destination. Another notable site is the Leifeng Pagoda, which offers panoramic views of West Lake and the surrounding landscape. If you're a tea lover, Hangzhou is also the birthplace of China's famous Longjing (Dragon Well) tea, and you can visit tea plantations on the hills surrounding the city to learn about the tea-making process and enjoy a freshly brewed cup of this world-renowned green tea.

To get to Hangzhou from Shanghai, you can take a high-speed train from Shanghai's Hongqiao Station, which takes around an hour and a half. Once you arrive, West Lake is just a short distance from the station, and you can easily explore the area by foot, bike, or boat. The best time to visit Hangzhou is in the spring or autumn when the weather is pleasant and the scenery is at its most captivating. West Lake in particular is stunning during these seasons, with the cherry blossoms in spring and the colorful autumn foliage creating a picturesque backdrop.

ACCOMMODATION OPTIONS

Luxury Hotels

International Chains with Skyline Views: You can't talk about luxury in Shanghai without mentioning the breathtaking views from international hotel chains like ***the Ritz-Carlton or the Mandarin Oriental***. One of the best spots to stay is the Ritz-Carlton Shanghai, located in the heart of the city at 1376 Nanjing Road West. With its panoramic views of the Huangpu River and the stunning skyline, this hotel is an icon of luxury. The Ritz offers impeccable service, from the opulent rooms and suites that feature plush furnishings and marble bathrooms to the Michelin-starred restaurants on-site. The hotel boasts a rooftop bar that overlooks the city's skyline, making it a prime location to sip a cocktail while watching the lights twinkle on the famous Oriental Pearl Tower. Whether you're traveling for business or leisure, the Ritz-Carlton offers an unrivaled blend of luxury, comfort, and sophistication.

Booking a room at the Ritz-Carlton usually requires a minimum of two nights' stay, with prices starting at around $300 per night for a standard room. If you want to splurge, suites with city views can go upwards of $1,500 per night, especially during peak seasons. The hotel is located just a short walk from Shanghai's main shopping area on Nanjing Road and a quick taxi ride to the Bund, which is ideal for tourists looking to experience both the modern and historical sides of the city. You can easily book online through the Ritz-Carlton website or through popular hotel booking platforms like Booking.com. One downside, however, is the price—while the luxury is unmatched, it's not a budget-friendly option for everyone.

Mandarin Oriental Pudong: Another must-visit luxury hotel with incredible skyline views is the Mandarin Oriental in Pudong, located at 111 Jincheng Road. This hotel stands as a monument to modern elegance, with its sleek glass exterior and spacious, high-end interiors. Each room offers spectacular views of the Huangpu River, the Lujiazui financial district, and the sprawling city below. The Mandarin Oriental is known for its stellar service, and its expansive spa, which is one of the best in the city, provides the ultimate in relaxation. The hotel also boasts multiple fine dining options, including the Michelin-recommended restaurant, Yong Yi Ting, where you can indulge in the finest Chinese cuisine.

Prices here vary, but expect to pay around $400–$500 per night for a standard room. Like the Ritz, the Mandarin Oriental offers a range of suites that can go for over $1,000 per night during peak seasons. While the hotel is a bit farther from the traditional heart of Shanghai, its location in Pudong puts you close to the financial district and the iconic Shanghai Tower. The Mandarin is easily accessible by taxi or metro, but the downside is that the Pudong area can feel a bit more corporate and less charming than the city's historic areas like the Bund or the French Concession.

Mid-Range Hotels

*Comfortable and Affordable Options in the City Cente*r: If you want to stay in the heart of Shanghai without splurging on a luxury hotel, there are several great mid-range hotels that will make you feel right at home while keeping costs reasonable.

Holiday Inn Shanghai Pudong, located at 899 Dongfang Road, Pudong. This hotel is perfect for travelers who prefer a quieter, more peaceful stay, yet still want to be close to the action. Positioned in the financial district of Pudong, it offers a blend of comfort and modern amenities. The rooms are spacious and feature contemporary furnishings, with panoramic views of the city's skyline, making it a great spot to unwind after a busy day of sightseeing. The hotel also has a range of dining options, including a casual cafe and an upscale Chinese restaurant, so you'll never have to go far for a satisfying meal.

The pricing at the Holiday Inn Shanghai Pudong is quite reasonable, with rates for a standard room starting around $100 per night. During peak tourist seasons, like Chinese New Year or summer months, prices can go up to around $150 per night for a standard room. It's easy to book through the official Holiday Inn website or third-party booking platforms like Expedia or Booking.com. The hotel is easily accessible by public transport, with the closest metro station being the *Century Avenue* station (Line 2, 4, 6, and 9), just a 5-minute walk away. One downside is that while the hotel provides a comfortable stay, it lacks some of the extra luxury touches you'd find in higher-end hotels, such as a rooftop bar or an expansive spa. But for those who prioritize location and practicality, it's an excellent choice.

Motel 168, located at 335 Changde Road in the heart of the city. Motel 168 is known for providing affordable yet high-quality accommodations, with comfortable rooms, friendly service, and an excellent central location. This hotel is especially ideal if you're traveling on a budget but still want to be close to popular attractions like People's Square, Nanjing Road, and The Bund. Rooms are simple yet stylish, with modern amenities like free Wi-Fi, air conditioning, and flat-screen TVs.

Booking a room at Motel 168 is incredibly affordable, with rates starting around $60 per night for a basic room. Prices can increase slightly during busy seasons but rarely exceed $100. It's a great value for the price, especially given the prime location. Getting there is easy—**People's Square** metro station (Line 1, 2, and 8) is just a short walk away, making it easy to navigate Shanghai's attractions. While the hotel offers limited services compared to larger chains, it's a great option for budget-conscious travelers who are mainly looking for a clean, comfortable place to rest at night. One downside, though, is that the hotel doesn't have a fitness center or any significant additional amenities. Still, for those who are more focused on exploring the city than lounging in the hotel, Motel 168 is a perfect pick.

Family-Friendly Hotels Near Attractions: Traveling with the family? Shanghai has plenty of family-friendly hotels that offer convenience and comfort, all while being close to major attractions. ***The Novotel Shanghai Atlantis***, located at 728 Pudong Avenue in the Lujiazui area, is one such hotel. This 4-star hotel is ideal for families who want to be near top attractions like the Shanghai Science and Technology Museum, Oriental Pearl TV Tower, and Century Park. The hotel features spacious rooms with modern amenities like mini-fridges, free Wi-Fi, and flat-screen TVs, making it a comfortable base for families.

One of the best things about the Novotel Shanghai Atlantis is its location—just a short metro ride to the heart of the city, but away from the busy crowds. It's also incredibly family-friendly, with an indoor swimming pool, a children's play area, and even a kids' menu at the on-site restaurant. Room rates are reasonably priced, starting at $120 per night for a standard room, and can go up to $200 per night for family suites or rooms with city views. The Novotel Shanghai Atlantis can be booked directly via their website or through popular booking sites like Hotels.com. While the hotel offers many amenities, including a fitness center, the downside is that the pool is a bit smaller compared to higher-end hotels, so it can get crowded during peak times. But overall, it's an excellent choice for families looking for a balance of comfort and convenience.

Another great family-friendly option is the ***Ramada Plaza Shanghai,*** located at 2000 Yan'an Road West. This mid-range hotel provides spacious rooms and family suites equipped with everything you need for a comfortable stay, including kitchenettes, which is ideal for long stays or those with young children. The hotel's location near Jing'an Temple is convenient for those looking to explore a mix of modern and traditional Shanghai, and it's also near several family-friendly attractions, such as Shanghai Zoo and Shanghai Museum. The hotel's restaurant serves both local and international dishes, so you won't have to worry about meal options for the little ones.

Room rates at the Ramada Plaza Shanghai start at $90 per night for standard rooms, with family suites costing around $160 per night. The hotel is easily accessible by metro, with the **Jing'an Temple** station just a short walk away. The downside is that the hotel is located slightly further from the waterfront area and the Bund, so it may require a longer travel time to visit some of Shanghai's iconic landmarks. However, for those who prefer a quieter, more residential area, the Ramada is a great choice.

Budget-Friendly Stays

If you're a backpacker or a solo traveler seeking to meet like-minded people, staying in a *hostel* is a great way to save on accommodation while immersing yourself in the local culture. One of the top budget-friendly hostels in Shanghai is the

The Captain Hostel, located at 56 Yongjia Road, in the French Concession area. This hostel is a favorite among travelers for its laid-back, friendly vibe and excellent location.

The Captain Hostel offers both dormitory-style rooms and private rooms, making it an ideal option for solo travelers or those traveling in groups. The hostel's common areas are spacious, with a cozy lounge where guests can relax, share travel stories, or mingle over a drink at the bar. The highlight of this place is its unbeatable location – just a short walk away from **Xintiandi** and **Tianzifang**, two of Shanghai's most popular cultural and entertainment districts.

Room rates at The Captain Hostel are highly affordable, with dormitory beds starting at just $15 per night, and private rooms available for around $50 per night. The hostel also offers amenities like free Wi-Fi, a fully equipped kitchen for guests to prepare their own meals, and an in-house cafe serving delicious local and international food. One downside, however, is that the shared bathrooms can be a bit small and crowded during peak hours. Still, for backpackers looking for an affordable, social place to stay, The Captain Hostel is an excellent choice. Booking is easy through platforms like Hostelworld or Booking.com, and the staff is incredibly friendly and helpful, making your stay in Shanghai even more enjoyable.

For those who prefer a quieter, more intimate stay in a traditional neighborhood, *guesthouses* offer an ideal balance of affordability and authenticity. One standout guesthouse is **Shanghainese Guesthouse,** located in Fuxing East Road, a charming street in the French Concession. This cozy guesthouse gives you the opportunity to experience Shanghai as a local, with its traditional decor, warm atmosphere, and close proximity to some of the city's most beloved cultural sites, including The Bund, Jing'an Temple, and People's Square. The guesthouse offers private rooms that are simple but cozy, complete with essential amenities like air conditioning, free Wi-Fi, and a small desk for those who might need to catch up on some work or journaling. The owners are extremely friendly and often offer insider tips on what to do and see around the city, providing a more personalized touch than you'd get at larger hotels.

Room rates at the Shanghainese Guesthouse are incredibly affordable, starting at $40 per night for a standard room, and around $70 per night for a larger room or suite. For a private guesthouse experience in the heart of one of Shanghai's most charming neighborhoods, this is an unbeatable price. The downside to staying here is that it's a small, family-run establishment, so the rooms are fairly basic compared to other types of accommodations. The guesthouse also has limited facilities compared to larger hotels, such as no on-site restaurant or gym. However, its intimate setting and authentic atmosphere make it a great option for travelers looking for a peaceful and personal stay in Shanghai's historical core. Booking is straightforward via platforms like Agoda or through the guesthouse's own website.

If you're looking for something a bit more unique, *the Mingtown Nanjing Road Youth Hostel* is another excellent budget option located at No. 58, West Nanjing Road, right in the center of Shanghai's shopping and business district. This hostel offers a variety of room options, from budget-friendly dorms to more private, comfortable rooms. The Mingtown Hostel stands out for its eclectic vibe, combining modern conveniences with elements of Chinese culture, making it a great place for travelers who want to experience Shanghai's blend of old and new. The location couldn't be more convenient, with the iconic Nanjing Road and the People's Square metro station just steps away, making it a perfect base for exploring the city's top attractions like The Bund, Yu Garden**, and the Shanghai Museum.

Dormitory rooms at Mingtown Hostel start at around $12 per night, and private rooms can be booked for as little as $40 per night. The hostel is also home to a cozy common area where you can meet fellow travelers and share experiences, as well as an on-site café offering both Chinese and Western dishes. Guests can also enjoy a nice view of the city from the rooftop, making it a pleasant place to unwind after a day of sightseeing. One downside, however, is that the hostel's facilities, such as the bathrooms, can sometimes get crowded during peak travel seasons, especially when the hostel is fully booked. Despite this, Mingtown Hostel offers fantastic value for its prime location and friendly atmosphere. Booking can be done easily on sites like Hostelworld or directly through the hostel's website.

For travelers who want an even more affordable option, the **Shanghai Rock & Wood International Youth Hostel**, located at No. 18, Xinle Road in the French Concession, is another popular choice. This hostel is a hidden gem, offering a quiet escape from the city's fast pace while being just a short distance from many major attractions. The rooms are clean and basic, with the option for dorms or private rooms, and you can enjoy amenities like free Wi-Fi, a communal kitchen, and a comfortable lounge area where you can relax and socialize with other guests. The staff here is known for being incredibly friendly and knowledgeable, providing tips on how to explore the city on a budget.

The pricing is extremely affordable, with dormitory beds starting at just $10 per night, and private rooms available for around $35. While the hostel doesn't offer as many luxury amenities, its location and the quality of the service make it a top contender for budget travelers. The downside, of course, is the lack of a gym or restaurant, which may be a dealbreaker for some, but for those who simply need a clean and safe place to sleep after a long day of sightseeing, Rock & Wood is an excellent choice. Booking is available on Hostelworld or directly through the hostel's website.

DINING AND CUISINE

Traditional Shanghai Cuisine

One of the most famous dishes in Shanghai is the *Xiaolongbao*, or soup dumplings. These delicate little dumplings, typically filled with pork and a savory broth, have become an international sensation, and for good reason. The moment you take a bite, the soup inside bursts out, and you're met with a perfect balance of rich broth and tender meat. The secret to a good Xiaolongbao lies in its balance—too much broth can make it soggy, and too little will make it dry. The dough should be thin yet resilient enough to hold the filling without breaking under pressure. While many eateries in Shanghai serve this beloved dish, there are a few spots that are known for making the best. One such place is **Din Tai Fung**, located at No. 168, Lujiazui Road, Pudong, which has garnered a reputation for serving consistently excellent soup dumplings. Another spot, the legendary Nanxiang Steamed Bun Restaurant, located in the Yuyuan Garden, is often considered the birthplace of *Xiaolongbao*. Prices typically range from ¥40-¥80 for a basket of these delicious dumplings, depending on the place and size. For those who want a bit of a splurge, the Shanghai Tower's top floor has a stunning panoramic view, paired with exquisite soup dumplings at one of its fine dining establishments. For an authentic experience, try to go early in the morning when the dumplings are freshly made and served piping hot.

Another dish that is a true seasonal delicacy in Shanghai is the **Shanghai Hairy Crab**. Every year, from October to December, these crabs are caught fresh from the Yangcheng Lake, located just outside the city, and they become a highly anticipated feature on the local food scene. Known for their sweet, tender meat and rich roe, **Hairy Crabs** are a must-try for any foodie visiting Shanghai during this time. The crabs are typically steamed and served with ginger vinegar to accentuate their flavor. Eating **Hairy Crab** is an experience in itself—there's something ceremonial about cracking open the shells and savoring the rich roe. One of the best places to try this seasonal delight is **Yang Cheng Lake Crab Restaurant**, located at No. 41, Yuyuan Road, Huangpu District. The restaurant offers a menu entirely dedicated to Hairy Crab, with a variety of preparation methods and dipping sauces. The price of a single Hairy Crab can range from ¥150-¥300, depending on the size and season, but it's worth every penny. Don't forget to pair the crab with a cup of Shaoxing wine to enhance the meal. While the crabs are a seasonal treat, they are so ingrained in the culture that you'll often see them on the menu from autumn onwards, whether at dedicated crab restaurants or at high-end hotels that serve this delicacy as part of a multi-course meal.

Red-Cooked Pork is another classic Shanghai dish that you must try when visiting. Also known as **Hong Shao Rou**, this dish is made by braising pork belly in a sweet, soy-based sauce with hints of star anise and ginger. The pork is slow-cooked until it's melt-in-your-mouth tender, with the fat softening into a luscious, silky texture. The rich, caramelized sauce coats each piece of meat, creating a savory-sweet dish that is perfect with a bowl of steaming rice. Red-Cooked Pork is a staple in traditional Shanghai cooking, and it is often found in family-run restaurants as well as upscale eateries.

One of the most famous places to enjoy this dish is Lao Zheng Xing, located at No. 108, Fuzhou Road, Huangpu District. This restaurant, one of Shanghai's oldest, has been serving up Hong Shao Rou since 1910 and is a beloved spot among locals. The dish can be ordered for as little as ¥60-¥100 per serving, making it an affordable yet indulgent treat. The restaurant also serves other traditional Shanghai dishes, but their Hong Shao Rou is the true star of the menu. It's a comforting dish that reflects the warmth and heartiness of Shanghai's food culture, perfect for a leisurely meal with family or friends.

For a more upscale experience of Red-Cooked Pork, head to The Bund, where some high-end restaurants feature their take on this classic. M on the Bund at No. 5, The Bund, is one of the city's most well-regarded restaurants for innovative takes on traditional Shanghai fare, including Hong Shao Rou. Here, you can savor a gourmet version of the dish, where the flavors are deepened, and the presentation elevated, for around ¥120-¥180 per serving. Whether you're dining in a family-run eatery or enjoying a refined version at a luxurious restaurant, Red-Cooked Pork is a dish that brings a taste of Shanghai's culinary roots to life in every bite.

Street Food Scene

One of the most thrilling aspects of Shanghai's street food scene is the vibrant night markets that come alive as the sun sets. These markets are more than just places to buy food—they're a cultural experience in themselves. As night falls, the streets fill with the rich aroma of grilling meats, simmering soups, and freshly made dough. A favorite night market among locals and tourists alike is *Dongtai Road Antique Market in the Old City.* While the market is known for its antique stalls, it's the nearby street food vendors that draw the real crowds.

Here, you'll find everything from *stinky tofu* a local delicacy with a pungent smell that hides a delicious taste to *grilled skewers* of lamb, beef, and seafood. Each vendor specializes in their own specialty, ensuring that the offerings are fresh and flavorful. The prices are reasonable, with most snacks ranging from ¥10 to ¥30. If you're feeling adventurous, don't miss out on the deep-fried buns stuffed with juicy pork or the xiaolongbao (soup dumplings) sold on the street, which might just rival the best in the city's upscale restaurants.

Another must-visit night market is the **Wujiang Road Food Street,** located in the Jing'an District, a narrow pedestrian street filled with food stalls offering a diverse range of Shanghai's favorite street eats. It's an ideal spot to try *shengjianbao*, pan-fried pork dumplings that are crispy on the bottom and juicy inside, or a plate of *chuan (skewered meats*) seasoned with aromatic spices. For around ¥15-¥40 per dish, you can indulge in the comfort of Shanghai's finest street food. The ambiance is electric, and the vibrant energy of the crowds will transport you straight into the heart of local culture. Whether you're people-watching or trying new dishes, the Wujiang Road Food Street offers a full Shanghai experience.

If you're an early riser and want to get a taste of the local breakfast specialties, Shanghai has a whole other world of delicious street food waiting for you. Breakfast in Shanghai is a serious affair, and one of the most beloved morning treats is **jianbing**, a crispy, savory crepe filled with eggs, herbs, and a variety of fillings like pickled vegetables or spicy sauces. Street vendors can be seen at nearly every corner, griddling these hot crepes fresh in the mornings, often served with a crispy fried **youtiao** (fried dough stick) to dip inside. The combination of the slightly sweet crepe, the crunchy dough stick, and the array of fresh fillings creates a truly satisfying start to the day. **Jianbing** is a popular breakfast choice for locals, and the vendors usually set up shop near busy metro stations or popular street corners in the **Puxi area**. A typical serving of **jianbing** can cost anywhere from **¥6 to ¥15**, depending on the location and fillings, making it a budget-friendly yet immensely flavorful breakfast option.

For those seeking an even more authentic breakfast experience, *youtiao* (fried dough sticks) is another beloved choice. These long, golden, crispy sticks of dough are often enjoyed with a cup of *soy milk or conge* (rice porridge). You can find youtiao served in many of the same breakfast stalls where jianbing is made, but sometimes they're sold on their own, perfect for dipping into warm soy milk or as an accompaniment to other dishes. One of the best places to grab youtiao is at Lao Yu's Breakfast Stall, located at No. 288, Zhaojiabang Road, Xuhui District. Here, the youtiao is fried to perfection and served with a choice of traditional dips. Expect to pay around ¥5-¥10 for a serving of this crispy treat.

As you wander through the streets of Shanghai, the food stalls tempt you with tantalizing aromas and vibrant sights that make it impossible to resist trying a little bit of everything. If you find yourself at Xintiandi, an upscale neighborhood in the Huangpu District, be sure to check out the street food stalls along Madang Road. Although this area is known for its trendy shops and modern architecture, you can still find traditional Shanghai snacks like *chicken feet, fish ball*s, and *stir-fried noodles*. These stalls offer a perfect fusion of old and new, with traditional snacks presented with a modern twist. The price range for these items is usually ¥10 to ¥25, which makes it an affordable yet satisfying stop during your exploration of the city.

Fine Dining and International Cuisine

Ultraviolet by Paul Pairet, located at No. 1-3, Dongping Road, Xuhui District. Ultraviolet has earned three Michelin stars, and for good reason—it's not just a restaurant, but a multisensory experience. The 10-seat venue offers a one-of-a-kind culinary journey, where each course is paired with visual, auditory, and olfactory cues, creating an immersive environment that makes dining here a truly unique experience. Booking a table requires advance reservations (usually months in advance) and comes with a hefty price tag of approximately ¥3,000-¥5,000 per person, but the memories will be worth every penny. Ultraviolet is an exclusive gem that promises not just a meal, but a profound exploration of flavors, textures, and emotions.

Another gem in Shanghai's Michelin crown is ***Jade on 36*** at the Pudong Shangri-La Hotel. With panoramic views of the city's skyline and the Bund, this restaurant combines high-end French and Chinese fusion cuisine to create a visually stunning and flavor-packed experience.

The panoramic view from the restaurant offers an unbeatable backdrop as you enjoy dishes like pigeon with foie gras or lobster with ginger and lemongrass. The tasting menu here ranges from ¥1,000-¥1,800 per person, and it's a treat for anyone looking to enjoy both top-tier food and stunning views. For special occasions, the private dining rooms provide an added touch of exclusivity, ensuring that every dinner is as memorable as the last.

Another popular restaurant for fusion food is *T8 Restaurant and Bar*, located at No. 8, Zhongshan East 1st Road, Huangpu District. The restaurant is known for its distinctive

blend of Asian flavors and European technique, creating dishes like Peking duck with a soy glaze**, Japanese sushi rolls with French foie gras, and a variety of tapas-style small plates. The ambiance here is lively and modern, with floor-to-ceiling windows offering a dramatic view of the skyline. T8 is known for its creative cocktails, which pair perfectly with the restaurant's dynamic menu. A meal here typically costs between **¥400-¥800** per person, making it a fantastic choice for anyone looking to explore innovative flavors while enjoying a laid-back yet upscale vibe.

If you're in the mood for Japanese cuisine, *Sushi Oyama*, located at No. 61, Fenyang Road, Xuhui District, is a must-visit. It's an intimate, quiet sushi restaurant with an emphasis on the finest ingredients, perfect for those who appreciate the artistry of sushi. The chef uses only the freshest, seasonal fish, and every piece of sushi is meticulously crafted. Expect to pay between ¥800-¥1,500 per person for a full sushi tasting experience. The personal service and refined atmosphere elevate the experience, making it one of Shanghai's top sushi destinations.

For lovers of Italian food, *La Scala* in the JW Marriott Hotel Shanghai, located at 399 Nanjing West Road, Huangpu District, is a luxury dining destination that brings a taste of Italy to the heart of the city. The restaurant offers a beautiful view of the city's skyline while serving Italian classics such as risotto with truffle, lobster pasta, and a range of fine wines from Italy's top vineyards. The cost here is a bit steep, typically ranging from ¥500-¥1,200 per person, but the combination of quality ingredients, an elegant setting, and impeccable service make it a top choice for food lovers.

Tea Houses and Dessert Spots

When it comes to traditional Chinese tea ceremonies, one place that captures the essence of this centuries-old practice is *Huxinting Teahouse*, located in the heart of Yu Garden (No. 218, Anren Street, Huangpu District). This iconic teahouse is a must-visit for anyone wanting to experience the calm, meditative quality of tea culture. Built in the Ming Dynasty, the teahouse stands on stilts over a pond, offering a serene escape from the bustle of the city. The ceremony here is an art form; skilled tea masters prepare the tea in intricate steps, explaining the significance of each stage, from selecting the leaves to the precise brewing technique. It's not just about drinking tea—it's about understanding the philosophy behind it. The experience includes a variety of teas, such as **Longjing** and Tie Guan Yin, served with delicate snacks like pine nut cakes.

Tea sets are priced between ¥100-¥300 per person, depending on the package. It's a perfect place for visitors who want to immerse themselves in traditional Chinese culture while enjoying a peaceful moment in one of Shanghai's oldest tea houses.

If you're looking for a more modern tea house experience, *The Tea Room by Yixing* (No. 202, Fuxing Road, Xuhui District) offers a contemporary twist on the tea ceremony. This place specializes in a curated selection of artisan teas from around China, with a sleek, minimalist decor that evokes tranquility while maintaining a modern flair. The tea ceremony here is a less formal, yet still highly respectful, presentation. Tea is served in small glass teapots with a refined, personal touch—perfect for tea lovers who are curious about the nuances of flavor but prefer a more relaxed setting.

The Oolong and Puer teas are particularly popular, often paired with their house-made pastries. The ambiance is cozy and quiet, ideal for anyone looking to escape the city's hustle and bustle for a moment. Prices vary from ¥80-¥200 for a tea set, and the service is impeccable, making it a perfect spot for a tranquil afternoon.

If you find yourself craving something a little more indulgent, *The Cheesecake Factory* (No. 1, Jinling East Road, Huangpu District) offers a mix of classic and contemporary desserts in an upscale setting. Known for its indulgent New York-style cheesecakes, this American import has become a favorite for those looking to enjoy rich, creamy desserts in the heart of Shanghai.

Their signature white chocolate caramel macadamia cheesecake is a must-try, while the raspberry lemon cheesecake offers a tart contrast to the richness of the cream cheese base. The Cheesecake Factory in Shanghai offers the same extensive dessert menu as their global locations, so whether you prefer a decadent slice of cheesecake or a lighter option like their lemon meringue pie, there's something for everyone. Prices are on the higher end, with most desserts priced between ¥60-¥150, but the portions are generous, and the quality is consistent.

For something more casual but still delightful, *Muffin Lab* (No. 234, Nanjing West Road, Jing'an District) is a quirky cafe that serves up artisanal muffins and cupcakes. With flavors like black sesame and red bean, chocolate matcha swirl, and baked cheesecake muffins, the selections here are both unique and mouthwatering. This cafe is a favorite among locals, offering a cozy, laid-back atmosphere that encourages you to stay and enjoy your treats. Muffin Lab also caters to dietary preferences with gluten-free and vegan options available. Desserts here are priced reasonably, from ¥30-¥60 per muffin or cupcake, making it a great stop for a sweet snack while exploring the city.

Top Restaurants and Food Markets

Lao Wang Ji, located at No. 173, Yuyuan Road, Huangpu District, is a beloved institution that's been serving up traditional Shanghai-style dim sum and **soup dumplings (xiaolongbao) for decades. The simple wooden tables, the constant chatter, and the sounds of sizzling woks make this place feel alive with history. The restaurant's xiaolongbao are the highlight, with a perfectly thin, delicate skin that encases a rich, savory broth. The price for a basket of these dumplings starts at around ¥30, and it's the ideal spot for those who want to dive straight into authentic, no-frills local dining.

Not far from the Yuyuan Garden, *Fengsheng Tang*, a small local joint located at No. 218, Yuyuan Street, offers Shanghai-style braised pork and other homey dishes that locals adore. The Hong Shao Ro (red-braised pork) is particularly popular here, known for its melt-in-your-mouth texture and rich, caramelized flavor that comes from hours of slow cooking. The environment is relaxed, with wooden tables and a bustling kitchen. This is an ideal stop for anyone wanting to sample Shanghai's unique take on pork dishes, with prices for most meals ranging from ¥40-¥100. Eating at local eateries like Fengsheng Tang is more than just about the food; it's about absorbing the history and stories that are etched into the walls and floors of these places.

As you venture further into Shanghai, the food markets become an integral part of the city's food culture. One of the most iconic food markets is *The City God Temple Bazaar,* located near No. 249, Zhonghua Road, Huangpu District. The market is a sensory overload—colorful stalls, the smell of fresh seafood, and the hustle and bustle of vendors calling out to passing shoppers. Here, you can find everything from fresh seafood to pickled vegetables, as well as traditional Chinese snacks that have been prepared using recipes passed down for generations.

Prices vary widely depending on what you buy; a bowl of fresh, steaming jiaozi (dumplings) can cost ¥15-¥30, while exotic snacks like stinky tofu might be priced between ¥10-¥20. The atmosphere here is both chaotic and charming, making it an excellent place for adventurous eaters who want to sample street food or gather ingredients for a homemade feast.

Another bustling food market is **Tongchuan Road Seafood Market** (No. 1580, Tongchuan Road, Putuo District), where the freshest fish, crabs, and shellfish are brought in daily from Shanghai's coastal waters. Whether you're in the mood for live crabs, fresh fish, or seafood skewers, this market is a treasure trove of aquatic delights. Vendors at Tongchuan Road are known for their Hong Kong-style fish balls and shrimp dumplings that are prepared on-site. For those interested in preparing their own seafood feast, the market is the place to be—just pick out your fresh catch, and vendors will clean, cut, and prepare it for you. Prices here range widely, with fresh fish costing anywhere from ¥50-¥150 per kilogram, depending on the type.

For a more modern and trendy experience, Wujiaochang Food Market is where you can explore a mix of contemporary and traditional flavors. Located at No. 888, Wujiaochang Road, Yangpu District, this market is a popular destination for both locals and expats. From exotic fruits to artisanal Chinese sausages, pickled vegetables, and everything in between, this market provides a vibrant mix of old-world charm and new-age dining experiences. This is an excellent place for foodies to explore different tastes, purchase fresh ingredients, or even grab a quick meal from one of the food stalls. Prices are also quite reasonable here, with freshly made baozi (steamed buns) starting at around ¥10-¥25 each.

When it comes to dining in Shanghai, The Bund is home to some of the most luxurious and fine dining restaurants in the city. For those who are looking for an upscale experience while still staying close to the vibrant food scene of the city, M on the Bund is a must-visit. Located at No. 5, The Bund, Huangpu District, this restaurant offers an incredible view of the skyline and a sophisticated menu that blends local and international flavors. From their pan-seared foie gras to the rich Shanghai-style lobster, M on the Bund offers a fine dining experience that's complemented by impeccable service. The restaurant also offers a large wine list, with prices for a meal here averaging ¥300-¥600 per person. With a refined yet welcoming atmosphere, M on the Bund is ideal for those who want to enjoy Shanghai's culinary heritage in a contemporary, upscale setting.

If you're craving the flavors of authentic Cantonese cuisine, Jade Garden (No. 318, Xizang Middle Road, Huangpu District) offers a delightful array of dishes that will leave you craving more. This fine dining establishment specializes in dim sum, sizzling hot pots, and roast duck, all served with a touch of sophistication. One standout dish is the roast duck, which is perfectly crispy on the outside while remaining tender and juicy inside. A meal at Jade Garden can be a little on the pricier side, ranging from ¥200-¥500 per person, but the quality of the food and the elegant setting make it well worth the splurge. Jade Garden's location, just off the People's Square, makes it easily accessible for those staying in the city center.

THINGS TO DO AND OUTDOOR ACTIVITIES

Parks and Gardens

People's Square is located in the Huangpu District, right at the center of the city. The square is flanked by several cultural and historical institutions, including the Shanghai Museum, Shanghai Grand Theatre, and the Shanghai Urban Planning Exhibition Center, making it a central hub for both leisure and education. It's easily accessible by public transportation, with the People's Square metro station (Lines 1, 2, and 8) right beneath the square, which means you can simply hop off the subway and step into the lush green space. If you're traveling by taxi, it's only a short ride from Nanjing Road or The Bund, making it a central and convenient spot for both tourists and locals alike.

The park itself spans over 140,000 square meters and is designed with a large central lawn, fountains, beautifully manicured gardens, and walking paths. As you enter the park, you're greeted by lush trees, colorful flower beds, and expansive lawns that are perfect for a leisurely walk or a peaceful sit-down. There are areas dedicated to different types of plants and flowers, including seasonal displays that change throughout the year. In the spring, the square bursts into life with vibrant blossoms, while in the fall, the trees offer a golden canopy of leaves. The square has a serene atmosphere that invites you to slow down and appreciate the beauty of nature, even in the middle of a thriving metropolis like Shanghai.

One of the most popular features of People's Square is the People's Park, which is a part of the larger square. It's a haven for locals who enjoy coming here to exercise, practice tai chi, or simply relax. It's not uncommon to see groups of elderly people gathering in the mornings to practice their routines, and you'll likely see families enjoying a day out together. The park is also known for its artificial lake, where you can rent a pedal boat or simply sit by the water, watching the swans glide by. For a truly tranquil experience, find a quiet corner near the lake or under one of the many shaded trees, and let the noise of the city fade away. The garden is also home to several well-maintained pavilions and gazebos, making it an ideal spot to take a break and enjoy the scenery.

If you're a fan of traditional Chinese gardens, People's Square also has its own modest yet captivating traditional garden area, inspired by classical Chinese landscape design. As you stroll through this area, you'll encounter winding paths, small ponds, and unique stone formations that are a hallmark of traditional garden design. The subtle use of water features, strategically placed rocks, and pavilions gives the space a sense of harmony and peace. The entire park exudes a calming atmosphere that blends nature with the art of design. Whether you're interested in photography, nature walks, or just soaking in the serenity, you'll find plenty of inspiration here.

As for tickets and pricing, the good news is that entry to People's Square and its surrounding park is entirely free. You can visit the square and stroll around the park without having to pay any admission fees. This makes it an ideal spot for travelers on a budget who want to experience Shanghai's green spaces without spending a dime. Another appealing aspect of People's Square is its accessibility to surrounding attractions. Once you've finished strolling through the park, you can easily explore nearby attractions, all within walking distance. For instance, the Shanghai Grand Theatre is just a few steps away, and if you're a fan of modern architecture, you can admire its striking design. For art lovers, the Shanghai Museum is also right there, with its impressive collection of Chinese art and artifacts. If you're interested in local culture, you can even explore the Shanghai Urban Planning Exhibition Center, which showcases the city's fascinating history and future development plans. These nearby attractions offer a deeper dive into Shanghai's rich cultural heritage and its rapid transformation into a modern metropolis.

Huangpu River Cruise

Starting with the basics, the **Huangpu River** runs through the heart of Shanghai, dividing the city into two distinct areas: the historic Puxi district and the ultra-modern Pudong district. The river, which has been an essential part of Shanghai's growth and history, stretches for about 113 kilometers, but the section that cuts through the city center is the most celebrated. The view from the river is especially captivating because it gives you a complete picture of Shanghai's contrasting architecture. On one side, you'll see the grand colonial buildings along the Bund, and on the other, the futuristic skyline of Pudong, with its towering skyscrapers like the Shanghai Tower and the Oriental Pearl Tower.

The process of booking your cruise is relatively straightforward, and there are several ways you can go about it. If you're staying in one of the city's major hotels, most concierge services can help you book tickets for a Huangpu River cruise, ensuring a seamless experience. You can also book your tickets directly online through various platforms like Klook, TripAdvisor, or GetYourGuide. These platforms offer a variety of packages that include different types of cruises, depending on your preferences, budget, and the time of day you plan to go. If you prefer, you can even head straight to one of the many piers along the Huangpu River to purchase your tickets in person. Popular departure points for these cruises are located near the Bund, including the Shiliupu Wharf and Waitan Dock, which are easily accessible by taxi or metro.

For a daytime cruise, tickets typically range from ¥70 to ¥150 per person, depending on the type of boat and the cruise duration. These cruises usually last between 45 minutes and an hour, giving you plenty of time to take in the sights without feeling rushed. Evening cruises, on the other hand, tend to be a bit more expensive, with ticket prices starting at around ¥150 and going up to ¥300 for premium options. The evening cruises often include dinner or snacks, which can also increase the price, but they are worth the extra cost for the unforgettable night-time view of the city's skyline illuminated by thousands of lights. Keep in mind that booking a cruise that includes dinner or drinks will cost more, but these options often offer a more intimate, relaxed experience, perfect for couples or those looking for a special way to see the city.

If you're booking in advance online, many services will offer you a voucher or QR code, which you can use directly at the dock. Alternatively, if you prefer to wait until you arrive in Shanghai, you can still find tickets at the pier, though they may be subject to availability, particularly during peak seasons like the summer months or around Chinese holidays. Booking in advance is always a good idea if you're visiting during busy times, as some of the more popular evening cruises can sell out.

The daytime cruise is an excellent option if you want to experience Shanghai in full daylight. The city's bustling energy is palpable from the river, and the daylight allows you to capture the sharp contrasts between the old and new parts of Shanghai. As the boat glides along the river, you'll pass the historic Bund district, with its iconic colonial-era buildings that once housed banks, trading companies, and consulates. On the opposite shore, the sleek and futuristic towers of Pudong rise from the river, their towering heights and sharp angles giving the city a dynamic, modern vibe. The cruise will also take you past several key landmarks, including the Shanghai Tower, the Jin Mao Tower, and the Oriental Pearl TV Tower. For photographers, the daytime cruise offers clear, vibrant shots of the skyline, so be sure to bring your camera or smartphone.

The evening cruise, however, offers a completely different experience. As the sun sets and the city lights begin to twinkle, the view from the river becomes downright magical. Shanghai's skyline transforms into a glittering sea of lights, with the Bund's historic buildings illuminated in warm, golden hues and the futuristic towers of Pudong glowing in brilliant neon. The most striking aspect of the evening cruise is the light show. The skyscrapers on both sides of the river are bathed in lights, and if you're lucky enough to take the cruise during a special event or holiday, the light displays are even more spectacular. The boats themselves are well-lit, giving you a chance to take some breathtaking photos with the city lights reflecting off the water.

Most of the boats used for these cruises are well-equipped for comfort, with ample seating both inside and on the open-air deck. The open-air deck is where most passengers prefer to be, as it offers the best views and a cool breeze. On some cruises, especially during the day, the lower deck can be enclosed and air-conditioned, providing a comfortable spot if you want to escape the heat or take a break from the sun. In terms of services, some boats offer light snacks or drinks for purchase, while others may include a more extensive selection, including a full meal. These options are usually available on the evening cruises, where dinner can be enjoyed while you take in the mesmerizing views.

Once you've booked your cruise, arriving at the departure pier is straightforward. The main Shiliupu Wharf is just a short walk from East Nanjing Road and can be easily accessed by the Metro Line 2. The pier is well-signposted, and you'll likely find plenty of staff at the dock ready to assist you. If you're unsure of where to go, just ask anyone around – Shanghai is a cosmopolitan city, and many locals understand basic English. Keep in mind that, during peak hours, the lines can get long, so it's best to arrive at least 20-30 minutes before your scheduled departure.

Shopping in Shanghai

Nanjing Road is home to some of the most luxurious shopping destinations, where gleaming glass facades and towering buildings house renowned brands such as Louis Vuitton, Gucci, Chanel, and Prada. These are the epitome of upscale shopping in Shanghai, where prices can easily stretch into the thousands for a single piece. But it's not just about the brands – it's about the experience. Take a walk along Nanjing Road East to see the sheer volume of stores, from global high-street fashion chains to flagship stores of the most prestigious luxury labels.

You'll find Hysan Place, The IAPM Mall, and Plaza 66, each offering a world-class shopping experience, with a huge selection of luxury goods, accessories, cosmetics, and even fine dining options within their walls. The ambiance of these malls is chic, sophisticated, and global – offering an almost cinematic experience where you can browse to your heart's content or take in the view of the glistening city outside.

For an even more exclusive shopping experience, head to The Bund area, where you'll find the Waldorf Astoria Shanghai and nearby high-end department stores like Shanghai House of Fraser. These places offer a chance to immerse yourself in luxury shopping, as well as enjoy high-end services like personalized stylists and premium customer care. The level of service in these malls often includes concierge services, offering help with everything from booking private viewings to providing free delivery for purchases. If you're interested in high-end fashion, the malls around this area are perfect for you.

The process of shopping in these luxury malls is incredibly smooth. Most of the time, you can simply walk in, browse, and enjoy the spacious, air-conditioned environment. If you want to make a purchase, it's as easy as picking out your item, taking it to the counter, and paying with cash, credit card, or mobile payment apps like Alipay or WeChat Pay. For international visitors, most stores will have staff who can communicate in English, and some even offer tax-free shopping, which can make your purchase a bit sweeter. The price range for shopping in these areas varies widely. You can expect to pay anywhere from ¥500 for smaller accessories like scarves and sunglasses to well over ¥10,000 for a luxury handbag or piece of jewelry. While it's easy to get lost in the glittering displays, it's also worth remembering that Shanghai is a city where you can negotiate. In some of the smaller stores or street vendors, there's room for bargaining, though it's rare in the high-end malls.

But if you're looking for something more authentic, you can turn your attention to the local markets, where you'll find a different kind of treasure. Shanghai's street markets are filled with a variety of goods that are perfect for souvenirs, gifts, and keepsakes. Yuyuan Bazaar, located near the stunning Yuyuan Garden, is one of the most famous places to shop for local crafts, antiques, and traditional souvenirs. This vibrant market is a maze of narrow lanes and colorful stalls selling everything from handmade silk scarves to charming porcelain tea sets. It's a great place to explore, as the shopping experience itself is as much about the atmosphere as it is about the products. Here, you'll find stalls and shops selling lacquerware, wood carvings, hand-painted fans, Chinese calligraphy, and **jade jewelry. These items, often created by local artisans, are imbued with a sense of history and tradition. Prices for these handcrafted goods can range from ¥50 for a small souvenir to ¥2,000 or more for a high-quality jade pendant or antique item. Bargaining is common at places like this, and it's often expected to haggle a bit to get the best price.

So, if you're up for a bit of fun negotiation, Yuyuan Bazaar is the place to be.

For a completely different shopping experience, head to *Tianzifang*, an artsy district in the French Concession area. Unlike the polished malls, this area is filled with small boutiques, artisanal shops, and independent galleries selling handmade items, clothing, jewelry, and souvenirs. If you're in the mood for a relaxed shopping experience, Tianzifang offers a charming labyrinth of narrow lanes lined with quirky shops. The prices here can vary depending on the type of item, but in general, you'll find local handicrafts like embroidered fabrics, leather goods, and paintings at reasonable prices. Expect to pay ¥100-¥500 for most souvenirs, though higher-end items, like custom-made jewelry or silk clothing, can run a bit higher.

The process of shopping in these local markets is similar to that in the high-end malls: pick what you like, ask for the price, and pay either in cash or using mobile apps. However, the real difference lies in the negotiation process. In these markets, sellers expect to negotiate, and it's part of the fun. Don't be afraid to haggle a bit – the worst they can do is say no, and often you can get a better deal than the listed price.

If you're looking for something unique, Shanghai also offers a number of pop-up shops and concept stores. These are often located in the city's trendy neighborhoods, like Xintiandi or Fuxing Park, where artists and designers showcase their products in a more modern, minimalist setting. Here, you'll find everything from locally designed fashion to indie music records, handmade homeware, and art prints. These pop-up stores are great for discovering the cutting edge of Shanghai's creativity, and they offer a more intimate and personal shopping experience.

In terms of tickets and booking, there's no need to book anything in advance for most of Shanghai's shopping areas. Whether you're heading to a high-end mall or a local market, you can simply walk in and start exploring. However, if you're visiting a more popular area, especially during the peak shopping seasons like the Chinese New Year or Golden Week, you may want to arrive early to avoid the crowds. Some of the upscale stores might also offer VIP shopping experiences, which can include a private shopping assistant, access to exclusive items, and special discounts. These VIP experiences can often be arranged in advance by calling the store directly or asking your hotel concierge to help you book an appointment.

Family-Friendly Activities

Shanghai Disneyland, an experience that feels like stepping into a whole new world. Located in the Pudong District, this sprawling 963-acre park is the first Disneyland park to be built in mainland China. Its opening in 2016 made Shanghai one of the most sought-after destinations for families looking to enjoy all the magic and wonder of Disney with a unique Chinese twist. The park is divided into several themed areas, including Mickey Avenue, Gardens of Imagination, Fantasyland, Adventure Isle, and Tomorrowland, each filled with attractions, shops, and restaurants that bring Disney's characters and stories to life.

The process of visiting Shanghai Disneyland begins by purchasing tickets, which can be done through the official website, on-site at the park, or via mobile apps

like Alipay. For a full-day experience, you can opt for 1-day admission tickets which cost around ¥399 for children and ¥575 for adults. If you're looking for a VIP experience or planning to spend more time, consider a 2-day ticket, priced at approximately ¥799 for adults and ¥579 for children. There are also group discounts and packages that combine the theme park with other Shanghai attractions for a more comprehensive experience. Keep in mind that tickets for peak periods like Chinese New Year, Golden Week, or school holidays can sell out quickly, so it's a good idea to book in advance. If you are planning to visit during these times, buying tickets online ahead of time is highly recommended.

Shanghai Disneyland offers a range of activities that are designed to appeal to families. The Enchanted Storybook Castle stands at the heart of the park, and no trip to Disneyland is complete without seeing it. Inside, you'll find immersive exhibits where your kids can experience the magic of Disney tales, such as the adventure through the Sleeping Beauty Castle. As you explore the different lands, be sure to take the time to catch the Tarzan: Call of the Jungle"/stage show, a wonderful family-friendly performance full of acrobatics and adventure. Of course, no visit to Disney is complete without meeting beloved characters like Mickey Mouse, Elsa from Frozen, or the whole Toy Story gang. These character meet-

and-greets, photo ops, and themed parades make the experience feel as though your kids have stepped into their favorite Disney movies. For older kids or thrill-seekers, the park offers some heart-racing rides like Tron Lightcycle Power Run in Tomorrowland and Pirates of the Caribbean: Battle for the Sunken Treasure in Treasure Cove. These rides are immersive and use cutting-edge technology to create experiences that are fun for all ages. Shanghai Disneyland also boasts a Garden of Imagination, perfect for younger children with whimsical carousels and gentle boat rides. The park is accessible, and there are family-friendly amenities like strollers, nursing rooms, and food stations throughout the grounds.

The **Shanghai Ocean Aquarium** is another fantastic family-friendly attraction in the city. Located along the Bund, this massive aquarium offers an educational and fun experience for visitors of all ages. The aquarium is famous for its glass tunnel, which allows you to walk underneath a 155-meter-long tank filled with all sorts of aquatic life.

This is one of the longest underwater tunnels in the world, providing an incredible, 360-degree view of the fish and sea creatures swimming around you. It's not just a fun visual spectacle but also an educational opportunity, as the aquarium is home to over 450 species from both fresh and saltwater environments.

Getting to the Shanghai Ocean Aquarium is easy, as it's located near the East Nanjing Road Metro Station, which is just a short walk from Lujiazui, a bustling area of the city. The address is 1388 Lujiazui Ring Road, Pudong, and it's open daily from 9:00 AM to 6:00 PM. To visit, tickets can be purchased directly at the entrance or via their official website. The regular ticket price is approximately ¥160 for adults and ¥100 for children (aged 3-12). If you want to enhance your visit, there are also guided tours available, which can provide deeper insights into the aquarium's exhibits. Special tickets for educational programs and exhibitions are priced separately.

The Shanghai Ocean Aquarium is split into several themed sections, including The

Amazon Rainforest, The Coral Reef, The Polar Zone, and the Jellyfish Kingdom. Each section features an impressive variety of marine life. Kids will be fascinated by the seals and penguins in the Polar Zone, while the Amazon Rainforest exhibit showcases fascinating creatures like piranhas and alligator snapping turtles. There's also an incredible array of exotic fish and underwater species, such as sharks, stingrays, and giant squid. The aquarium also has a touch tank where children can interact with starfish, sea cucumbers, and other marine animals.

One of the highlights of the aquarium is the Shanghai Ocean Aquarium 4D Experience, a motion-sensory film that takes viewers on an underwater adventure. The film is both entertaining and informative, teaching children about marine conservation and the creatures that inhabit the world's oceans. Families can also enjoy the aquatic-themed gift shop, where you can buy plush toys, souvenirs, and educational materials to take home.

When it comes to booking tickets for both attractions, the process is relatively straightforward. For Shanghai Disneyland, visiting their official website or mobile apps gives you an easy platform for booking tickets, checking for special promotions, and securing reservations for popular attractions. The same goes for the Shanghai Ocean Aquarium, where tickets are available online, as well as on-site. If you're visiting both locations on the same day or as part of a broader Shanghai tour, some companies offer package deals that combine entrance fees and even transportation for a more convenient experience.

Relaxation and Wellness

One of the most culturally significant and popular wellness experiences in Shanghai is *traditional Chinese massage*, an ancient practice that has been passed down through generations. Often referred to as **Tui Na** or **Chinese therapeutic massage**, this treatment combines acupressure, kneading, rolling, and friction to stimulate energy flow (or Qi) throughout the body. The idea is to balance the body's vital forces, release tension, and improve overall health. Many local wellness centers and spas in Shanghai offer traditional Chinese massage as part of their menu, and it's one of the most affordable ways to experience authentic wellness treatments in the city.

For a truly immersive experience, head to a specialized massage parlor or foot reflexology center. Reflexology is a form of massage that focuses on applying pressure to specific points on the feet, hands, and ears, which correspond to different organs and systems in the body. It's believed to promote relaxation, improve circulation, reduce stress, and even aid digestion and detoxification. In Shanghai, you'll find countless places offering reflexology, from humble yet reputable spots in the French Concession to swanky salons in the heart of Pudong. One such place, Yu Massage, located in **Xuhui District, is known for its skilled therapists and serene atmosphere. A one-hour session here will set you back about ¥200-300 ($30-$45), depending on the type of massage you choose.

The process for booking a traditional Chinese massage in Shanghai is usually very straightforward. Most spas and massage parlors accept walk-ins, though it's a good idea to make a reservation, particularly if you're visiting during peak hours or weekends. You can book appointments in advance by calling or visiting the spa's website. Many venues also use WeChat for booking, making the process even more convenient for both locals and international visitors. For larger, more renowned spas, it's advisable to check availability and make an online booking through their official websites or apps to ensure you get the time slot you want.

If you're looking for a more refined, luxurious wellness experience, Shanghai boasts an impressive selection of luxury hotel spas that are perfect for those who want to relax in style. The city's high-end hotels, such as The Peninsula Shanghai, Mandarin Oriental, and the Waldorf Astoria Shanghai, feature world-class spas that offer a wide range of treatments, from deep tissue massages to anti-aging facials and wellness therapies inspired by both Eastern and Western practices. These spas often focus on holistic wellness, combining luxurious treatments with serene settings designed to calm the mind and body.

Take, for instance, The Peninsula Spa in The Peninsula Shanghai, which is a sanctuary of tranquility and elegance. Located along the Bund, this spa offers a range of treatments that combine ancient Chinese healing methods with modern luxury. Guests can enjoy massages using aromatherapy oils, facials using advanced skincare products, or even indulge in personalized spa journeys tailored to individual needs. The spa also has a hydrotherapy circuit with saunas, steam rooms, and plunge pools, making it the perfect spot to unwind after a long day of sightseeing or business meetings. For a two-hour signature treatment, expect to pay around ¥1,800 ($250), which is on the higher end, but the experience and relaxation are well worth it.

Another standout is the Mandarin Oriental Pudong, which boasts one of the most luxurious spa experiences in the city. The Mandarin Oriental Spa offers a fusion of Eastern healing traditions and Western techniques, with treatments designed to restore balance to the body and mind. Highlights include Shiatsu massages, rejuvenating facials, and reflexology sessions. The spa is known for its exceptional service and tranquil setting, with panoramic views of the Huangpu River and Pudong skyline, adding to the sense of escape. A signature two-hour treatment at this spa typically costs around ¥2,000 ($290), but you can also book packages or multiple treatments at discounted rates if you want to indulge in a full-day experience.

While these high-end hotel spas offer an incredible, upscale experience, there are also numerous mid-range spas across the city that provide great service and quality treatments at a more affordable price. For example, Dragonfly Therapeutic Retreat is a well-known spa chain in Shanghai that combines luxurious treatment rooms with professional therapists and a tranquil atmosphere. Locations across the city, including in Jing'an District and Xujiahui, offer everything from traditional massages to unique treatments like hot stone therapy and head, neck, and shoulder massages. The prices at Dragonfly are more accessible, with a one-hour traditional Chinese massage costing around ¥380-500 ($55-$70).

Booking a treatment at these spas is typically done through the spa's website, where you can check availability and make reservations. Most spas also accept walk-ins, but if you're traveling during peak times or public holidays, booking ahead is always a good idea. You can expect to pay a little more if you choose packages or add-on services, such as aromatherapy oils or scalp treatments, but the extra cost can significantly enhance your relaxation experience. You can pay with credit cards, WeChat Pay, or Alipay, which are commonly accepted at spas and wellness centers in Shanghai.

One of the major advantages of booking a spa experience in Shanghai is the convenience of the city's excellent transportation system. Whether you're staying in the Pudong District or the French Concession, getting to your wellness destination is easy, thanks to the city's well-connected metro lines and taxis. If you're staying at a hotel with a spa, the added bonus is that you don't even have to leave the building, which can be incredibly relaxing after a long day of touring the city.

For a more holistic wellness experience, some spas offer yoga or meditation classes as part of their services. These are perfect for those who want to reconnect with their inner self and find some peace amidst the busy city life. You can also find Tai Chi classes in some places, a traditional Chinese martial art that promotes relaxation, balance, and mental clarity. A one-hour Tai Chi class generally costs around ¥150-250 ($20-$35), depending on the location.

.

ART, CULTURE, AND ENTERTAINMENT

Museums and Galleries

China Art Museum, an iconic landmark in the heart of Shanghai's art district. Located in the Pudong area, the museum is housed in the impressive China Pavilion from the 2010 World Expo, a stunning example of modern architecture. The building itself is an architectural marvel with its red, inverted pyramid shape, making it hard to miss. If you're traveling by metro, take Line 8 and disembark at China Art Museum Station; the museum is directly across the street from the station, making it incredibly easy to access.

Inside, the China Art Museum features an extensive collection of Chinese contemporary art, with exhibitions that span both traditional and modern works. The museum showcases pieces from Chinese masters such as Zhang Daqian and Wu Guanzhong, as well as cutting-edge contemporary works that highlight the innovative nature of China's art scene today. The museum also hosts regular temporary exhibitions that explore various aspects of Chinese culture, including art, design, and technological advancement. Expect to see works that challenge conventional boundaries, often mixing modern techniques with traditional Chinese philosophies. It's a great place to discover new art while gaining a deeper understanding of China's artistic journey.

Admission to the China Art Museum is quite affordable. General entry costs around ¥30 ($4), though there are occasional special exhibitions that may have a higher entry fee. If you're planning on spending the entire day there or visiting more than once, you might want to inquire about any annual membership options that offer unlimited access to the museum and special exhibitions. The museum is open from 9:00 AM to 5:00 PM daily, with the exception of Mondays, when it's closed for maintenance. If you're a fan of contemporary art, mornings tend to be quieter, offering a more peaceful experience, especially if you prefer a more contemplative visit. Weekends can be busier, so arriving early is recommended to avoid the crowds.

Next, let's talk about the **Propaganda Poster Art Center**, a hidden gem nestled in the Jing'an District that offers a fascinating insight into China's political and cultural history. Tucked away on the second floor of a small building, this museum is dedicated to showcasing the history and evolution of propaganda posters from the Mao era (1949-1976). While it may not be as large as some of the city's more prominent museums, its unique focus on a specific period of Chinese history makes it a must-see for those interested in the interplay of art and politics.

Located at 868 Huashan Road, the museum is easily accessible via Line 2 of the metro, with Jing'an Temple Station being the closest stop. From there, it's about a 5-minute walk to the museum. Because of its more understated location, you might need to keep an eye out for the entrance, which is a small, inconspicuous door leading up to the museum on the second floor. Don't let the modest exterior fool you—inside, you'll find an incredible collection of vintage propaganda posters that reflect the Communist Party's campaigns, from the Great Leap Forward to the Cultural Revolution. The posters feature vibrant, often dramatic illustrations that were designed to inspire the Chinese people during pivotal moments in the country's history. Many of these posters are characterized by bold, idealized images of workers, soldiers, and peasants, all designed to embody the strength and unity of the Chinese people under the leadership of the Communist Party.

As you walk through the museum, you'll find yourself immersed in the political and social landscape of mid-20th-century China. The posters on display serve not only as pieces of art but also as propaganda tools—used to communicate messages about loyalty, discipline, and social change. The curator of the museum, a former collector of propaganda art, often gives visitors a deeper context for understanding these works. Some visitors find themselves particularly struck by the transformation of Chinese art during this period, from highly stylized depictions of national heroes to more abstract representations of everyday life.

What's particularly special about the Propaganda Poster Art Center is the opportunity to purchase some of these iconic prints for your personal collection. The posters for sale are reproductions, but they offer a lasting way to take home a piece of Chinese history. You can find posters ranging from ¥80-400 ($12-$60), depending on the size and rarity of the piece. The entry fee to the museum is also quite reasonable—¥30 ($4) per person, which makes it an accessible destination for both art lovers and those with a particular interest in China's historical period.

The Propaganda Poster Art Center is open daily from 10:00 AM to 6:00 PM, and it's best to visit in the morning or late afternoon to avoid larger crowds, especially on weekends. One unique aspect of the museum is the intimate, personal experience it offers. The smaller scale means there's less hustle and bustle, allowing you to engage deeply with the content and take your time exploring the posters. If you're interested in the historical context behind each piece, it's a good idea to visit with a guide, or ask the staff for additional insights into the posters' significance. There's also a gift shop where you can purchase books and memorabilia, making this a great place to find a unique souvenir that goes beyond the typical tourist offerings.

Both the China Art Museum and the Propaganda Poster Art Center reflect Shanghai's diverse artistic landscape—one embracing the global, contemporary future and the other offering a nostalgic, intimate look at China's past. If you're an art lover, or even just someone looking to better understand the cultural and historical forces that shaped modern China, these two museums are essential stops. The best part? They're located in neighborhoods that are perfect for exploration. After a visit to the China Art Museum, you can explore the nearby Century Park, Shanghai's largest green space, or stroll along the waterfront in the Pudong district, where you'll find stunning views of the city's skyline. Meanwhile, after visiting the Propaganda Poster Art Center, you can venture into the heart of Jing'an, a district that's full of cool cafes, shopping malls, and hidden gems.

Performances and Festivals

One of the must-see experiences for visitors to Shanghai is the exhilarating *Shanghai Acrobatic Show*. Shanghai's acrobatics tradition dates back to ancient times, and today, you can witness some of the world's most skilled performers at venues like the Shanghai Circus World. Located at 2266 Gonghe Xin Road in the Putuo District, this iconic venue hosts jaw-dropping acrobatic performances that include daring feats of flexibility, strength, balance, and coordination. If you're taking the metro, the Zhenping Road Station on Line 7 is the closest stop, from which it's a quick 5-minute walk to the venue. The Shanghai Acrobatic Troupe performs multiple shows a week, each lasting around 90 minutes, with both day and evening performances available. Ticket prices vary depending on your seat selection, with standard tickets starting at ¥200 ($28), while more premium options can run up to ¥500 ($70). This show is an absolute must-see for anyone visiting the city, and it's particularly great for families or anyone who loves watching skill and talent in its purest form. The acrobats, many of whom have been training since childhood, perform tricks that defy belief—such as human pyramids, contortionist displays, and cycling stunts that will leave you wide-eyed. The performances are a celebration of Chinese artistry and strength, offering a unique glimpse into a centuries-old tradition that has captivated audiences for generations.

Another exceptional cultural experience you can enjoy in Shanghai is the *Shanghai International Film Festival (SIFF)*, one of Asia's most prestigious cinematic events. Held annually in June, this festival is a showcase of international cinema, featuring hundreds of films from around the world, including top-tier blockbusters, cutting-edge independent films, and a selection of Chinese-language films. The Shanghai Grand Theatre, located at 300 Renmin Avenue, is the venue for many screenings, and it's a short walk from People's Square Station, which connects you to Lines 1, 2, and 8. Tickets for the film festival are generally priced between ¥50-200 ($7-$28), depending on the screening and venue, with special events and gala screenings sometimes reaching higher ticket prices. If you're planning to attend, it's a good idea to check out the festival schedule and book your tickets online in advance, as many screenings tend to sell out quickly, especially the more popular or award-winning films. Whether you're an avid cinephile or just someone looking to enjoy a night at the movies in one of China's most vibrant cities, the Shanghai International Film Festival offers something for everyone. It's a celebration of the art of filmmaking, drawing huge crowds of film lovers and professionals from across the globe. You'll have the opportunity to see the latest cinematic masterpieces, meet filmmakers, and participate in panel discussions and workshops. The festival is a perfect time to experience the global convergence of film culture in the heart of Shanghai.

If you're lucky enough to be in Shanghai during the *Lantern Festival*, you'll be treated to one of the most visually stunning and culturally rich events of the year. This festival marks the end of the Chinese New Year celebrations and is usually held on the 15th day of the lunar new year, which typically falls in February or March. The Lantern Festival in Shanghai is famous for its spectacular displays of illuminated lanterns,

representing everything from mythological creatures to cultural symbols. The best place to see these magical lanterns is at Yu Garden in the Old City, located at 218 Anren Street, just a short walk from Yuyuan Garden Station on Line 10. The festival typically runs from 6:00 PM to 9:00 PM each evening, with the lantern displays being most spectacular after dark. Admission to Yu Garden during the Lantern Festival is ¥40-80 ($6-$11), and the experience is absolutely unforgettable. As you wander through the garden, you'll be greeted by intricate lanterns hanging from trees, set along pathways, and displayed in large-scale installations. The atmosphere is magical, with the lanterns casting a warm glow over the historic garden, creating a dreamlike environment. If you're a photographer or just someone who enjoys a bit of spectacle, this is the time to visit. The Lantern Festival also features traditional performances such as lion dances, folk music, and food stalls selling delicious snacks. It's a vibrant celebration of Chinese culture and a fantastic way to immerse yourself in the local traditions.

In addition to the Lantern Festival, Shanghai celebrates the *Dragon Boat Festival* with much fanfare. Held annually in June, the festival commemorates the life and death of the ancient poet Qu Yuan. Dragon boat races are held across various parts of the city, but one of the most exciting places to witness these races is at the Zhouzhuang Water Town, a picturesque ancient water town located just a short drive from the city center. It's one of the most popular destinations for tourists during the Dragon Boat Festival.

To get there, you can take a direct bus or hire a private driver, which takes around 1.5 to 2 hours from central Shanghai. Admission to the races and surrounding festivities typically costs around ¥50-150 ($7-$21), depending on the location. The highlight of the Dragon Boat Festival is the actual race— teams of rowers race in beautifully decorated boats shaped like dragons. The energy is palpable, as spectators cheer on their teams while enjoying traditional foods like zongzi (sticky rice wrapped in bamboo leaves) and various other local delicacies. If you're in Shanghai during the Dragon Boat Festival, make sure to experience this vibrant, high-energy event that showcases the city's rich heritage and the competitive spirit of the local people.

Nightlife in Shanghai

Start your evening by heading to one of the city's most iconic spots: the Bund, the heart of Shanghai's historic waterfront. Here, you'll find an impressive array of rooftop bars that offer unparalleled views of the city's skyline. If you're someone who loves a great view, then a rooftop bar on the Bund is a must. Vue Bar at the Hyatt on the Bund (199 Huangpu Road) offers a sweeping panorama of both the Bund's colonial architecture and the gleaming futuristic towers of Lujiazui across the river. Getting to Vue Bar is simple: just hop off at East Nanjing Road Station (Lines 2 and 10) and take a 10-minute walk towards the river. The bar opens in the evening and stays open until 2:00 AM, so whether you're an early bird or a night owl, you can enjoy the view under the glow of Shanghai's dazzling lights. Expect to pay around ¥150-200 ($20-28) for cocktails, but with the stunning views and intimate atmosphere, it's well worth it. While Vue Bar is upscale, it's not excessively pretentious, making it a perfect place to start your evening in style. Sipping a well-crafted cocktail as you look out over one of the most breathtaking skylines in the world, you'll understand why the Bund is the symbol of Shanghai's charm and allure.

A more casual yet equally mesmerizing option on the Bund is The Roof at the Three on the Bund (3 Zhongshan Dong Yi Road). Located on the top of one of the city's most famous buildings, this bar is perfect for those who want to relax and enjoy a sophisticated atmosphere without the usual formality. Whether you're coming for a sundowner or to dance late into the night, this place is known for its laid-back ambiance, signature cocktails, and its sprawling views of the river and the city's famous skyline. The location itself is easy to find, and getting there from Nanjing East Road Station (Line 2) takes about 15 minutes on foot. Tickets or cover charges aren't usually required, though drinks here will set you back around ¥120-180 ($17-$25) per cocktail. The Roof is a great place to unwind with a drink in hand and enjoy the dynamic fusion of old and new Shanghai. As the night progresses, the atmosphere here evolves, shifting from a relaxed, classy vibe to a lively and buzzing crowd later in the evening.

For those looking to dance the night away, Shanghai's club scene is unparalleled, and one of the best neighborhoods to dive into the party scene is Xintiandi. Known for its fashionable, upscale bars and clubs, this area caters to both locals and expats who want to party until the early hours. M1NT is one of the most iconic nightclubs in Shanghai, and it's not hard to see why. Located at No. 318 Fuxing Road, M1NT is a multi-level, high-energy nightclub that draws an elite crowd with its sleek, contemporary design and top-notch service. If you're arriving via Xintiandi Station (Line 10), it's just a short walk from there. The club features a rooftop lounge, a dance floor, and even an aquarium in the middle of the club. The music is a mix of house, hip-hop, and EDM, with world-class DJs regularly spinning the decks. Entrance fees typically start at around ¥150 ($20) for general access, but they can rise for special events or guest DJs. Expect a crowd that's fashionable and ready to party. M1NT is one of the places in Shanghai where you'll see the city's most trendy locals and internationals mingling, so come prepared to socialize and dance.

If you're seeking a more intimate and music-centric experience, Shanghai has no shortage of jazz bars and live music venues where you can enjoy the local talent and relax in a dimly lit, atmospheric setting. JZ Club, located in Zhongshan Park at 46 Fuxing West Road, is one of the best spots for live jazz in Shanghai. The venue exudes the type of charm you'd expect from an iconic jazz bar, with its smooth ambiance, great acoustics, and stellar lineup of both local and international jazz acts. Getting to JZ Club is easy, as it's a short walk from Jing'an Temple Station (Lines 2 and 7). Tickets for shows are generally priced at ¥100-200 ($14-$28), with the price varying depending on the performer or event. This is the place to go if you want to experience Shanghai's thriving live music scene in a setting that feels both personal and professional. It's also a great spot to meet fellow music lovers, with an intimate vibe that lets you immerse yourself in the music. The club serves drinks and light bites, so you can sip on a cocktail while you enjoy the smooth sounds of the saxophone or piano. JZ Club is ideal for those who prefer the relaxed elegance of live jazz to the chaos of larger clubs.

For something a little more unconventional but equally engaging, consider visiting The Camel at 1/F, 120 Xintiandi North Block. It's not your average bar, but rather a laid-back haven for music lovers and backpackers alike, often featuring live indie and rock bands. The Camel's interior has a relaxed, pub-like atmosphere, and the music is always loud and energetic, providing a wonderful contrast to the city's ultra-modern nightclub scene. The vibe here is decidedly more chill, but no less fun. Drinks are reasonably priced, with beer starting at ¥30 ($4) and cocktails at ¥60-100 ($8-$14). The crowd tends to be younger and more eclectic, drawn by the relaxed vibe and the quality of live performances. This is a fantastic place if you're looking to discover new music, chat with locals, or just have a great time in a fun, low-key environment.

If you're a fan of speakeasy-style venues, you'll love the hidden gems scattered throughout Shanghai. One of the most famous spots is Bar Rouge located on the Bund at 18 Zhongshan Dong Yi Road. It's often ranked as one of the top bars in the city for its incredible rooftop view, creative cocktails, and intimate ambiance. Access to the venue feels exclusive, as it's tucked away behind an unmarked door in a stylish building. Inside, the décor mixes art-deco elements with modern flair, providing a sultry, glamorous atmosphere. Drinks here can be pricey, with cocktails ranging from ¥150-300 ($20-$42), but it's worth it for the view and the chic vibe. The nightlife here is sophisticated and trendy, with a crowd that appreciates the finer things in life.

Creative Hubs

Among the city's most compelling creative spaces are *M50 Art District* and Tianzifang, two areas where you'll discover everything from avant-garde galleries to quirky cafes and boutique shops, each contributing to the city's vibrant creative pulse. These are places where the creativity of Shanghai's past and present merge, giving both locals and visitors an enriching, stimulating experience. Whether you're a seasoned art lover or someone who enjoys wandering through places with a unique flair,

M50 and Tianzifang are must-visits for anyone wanting to explore Shanghai's thriving arts scene.

Your first stop should undoubtedly be the M50 Art District, located on 50 Moganshan Road**, in the Putuo District. M50 is Shanghai's equivalent of New York's Chelsea or London's Shoreditch—a former industrial area that's been transformed into a thriving contemporary art space. Getting to M50 is easy, especially if you're taking public transport. From Shanghai Railway Station, take Metro Line 4 and get off at Moganshan Road Station. It's only a five-minute walk from the station to the heart of the district. The area is free to roam, but if you want to check out the exhibits in the various galleries, most charge a small entrance fee—typically ¥20-40 ($3-$6). The best time to visit M50 is in the late afternoon or early evening, when the galleries start to bustle, but the crowds are still manageable, and the evening light adds a special quality to the area.

As you step into M50, the first thing that strikes you is the juxtaposition of old and new.

The former industrial buildings, with their exposed brick walls, steel beams, and large factory windows, now house over 100 art galleries, design shops, and artist studios. You can easily spend a few hours here, wandering from one gallery to the next. Expect to find a wide range of contemporary art styles—from bold, colorful paintings to photography, sculpture, and installations. The area has become a mecca for both established and emerging artists, with local Chinese artists showcasing works that reflect both the country's rich cultural history and its rapidly modernizing landscape. You might even catch an artist working in their studio, adding a sense of authenticity to the experience.

The galleries in M50 are as varied as the artworks themselves. Some focus on traditional Chinese themes with a modern twist, while others showcase more international styles, providing a fascinating blend of East and West. One of the standout galleries is Art+ Gallery, which often features cutting-edge works that push the boundaries of what art can be. Another must-see is Upstream Gallery, known for its innovative exhibitions that spotlight the avant-garde side of Chinese art. As you stroll, you'll also come across pop-up installations and quirky design shops, selling everything from locally-made jewelry and vintage prints to limited-edition artworks and eco-friendly products. If you're looking for a souvenir, this is a great place to find something truly unique that captures the creative spirit of Shanghai.

M50's cultural vibe extends beyond the art galleries. There are several cafes, bookshops, and small boutiques where you can pause, reflect, and recharge. One of the best spots to do so is Café M50, a charming little spot tucked away inside one of the galleries. Here, you can enjoy a warm cup of coffee while taking in the atmosphere of this creative hub. The café's industrial-chic aesthetic, with its minimalist decor and exposed brick, perfectly matches the vibe of the district. If you're lucky, you might even find an impromptu performance or exhibition happening, as the space is frequently used for events and creative gatherings.

After soaking in the artistic energy of M50, a short trip to *Tianzifang* is the perfect way to experience the more whimsical, eclectic side of Shanghai's creative scene. Located in the French Concession, Tianzifang is a labyrinth of narrow alleyways lined with artsy shops, quirky cafes, traditional courtyard houses, and boutique galleries. Getting to Tianzifang is easy, especially if you're coming from Xintiandi Station on Metro Line 10—just a short walk to the district. Tianzifang has become a hotspot for both locals and tourists, offering a perfect blend of old-world charm and modern creativity. The area is bustling with activity, particularly during weekends, when crowds flock to the area to browse its boutiques and sample its café offerings.

Tianzifang's charm lies in its ability to transport you to a different time while still showcasing Shanghai's contemporary culture. Unlike M50's larger galleries and artist studios, Tianzifang feels more like a traditional neighborhood that's been transformed by the creative spirit of its residents. The cobblestone streets and low-rise, old-style buildings provide a warm, intimate atmosphere, with street art and colorful murals adding a touch of flair to every corner. Unlike more commercialized shopping streets, Tianzifang retains an authenticity that invites visitors to explore, slow down, and appreciate the little details. It's the perfect place for aimless wandering, where every turn brings a new discovery.

Much like M50, Tianzifang offers a range of galleries, but these are often smaller and more focused on the intersection of art and lifestyle. You'll find a mix of contemporary art, vintage shops, fashion boutiques, and handcrafted homeware. If you're in the market for something uniquely Shanghai, look no further than the art galleries here, which often sell affordable prints and works by local artists. You might also find artisan shops offering handmade ceramics, textiles, or even custom-designed clothing—perfect souvenirs to remind you of the city's artistic pulse.

But beyond the art, Tianzifang is also known for its wide variety of cafes and eateries, making it the perfect spot to relax after a day of browsing. Whether you're in the mood for a traditional Chinese tea ceremony or a quirky café with a modern twist, you'll find plenty of choices. One of the best places to stop for a coffee is **Cafe de la Poste**, a cozy spot serving expertly brewed coffee and pastries in a vintage setting that feels straight out of a European café. If you're feeling adventurous, try **The Tap House**, a hidden gem offering craft beers from local breweries. The variety of dining options means that there's always something new to discover, from sweet treats to hearty meals.

For those who love to shop, Tianzifang is also home to an impressive array of unique boutiques and independent stores. If you're into fashion, you'll find stylish, locally-designed clothing that you won't find in the more commercial malls around Shanghai. If you're looking for home decor or gifts, you can browse through a collection of handpicked, one-of-a-kind items that reflect the creativity of the city's designers. Unlike larger shopping centers, these small shops are often run by local artisans, making your purchase feel more personal and connected to the community.

7-DAY ITINERARY

Day 1: Arrival and Orientation

Welcome to Shanghai, the shimmering metropolis where ancient traditions and futuristic innovation coalesce into an unforgettable experience. After your arrival, you'll quickly realize that this city isn't just a destination—it's a journey through history, culture, and modern marvels. The first day in Shanghai is all about getting acquainted with its energy, finding a sense of place, and immersing yourself in its iconic sights. From the comfort of your hotel to a leisurely evening stroll along the Bund, your first day will set the tone for the adventures ahead.

Morning: Check-In and Relaxation

Upon arriving at Shanghai Pudong International Airport (PVG), you'll likely be buzzing with excitement, eager to dive into the city. Depending on the time of your arrival, head straight to your hotel to check-in and drop off your luggage. If you've opted for a luxury stay, such as The Peninsula Shanghai or The Bund Riverside Hotel, you'll be welcomed by exceptional service and stunning views of the Huangpu River. For those looking for more budget-friendly options, there are plenty of mid-range hotels near People's Square or the French Concession area that offer both comfort and convenience.

Once you've checked in, it's time to relax and recover from your journey. Take some time to unwind in your hotel room, perhaps indulging in a brief nap or enjoying the views from your window. If you're staying in a luxury hotel, many of them have fabulous spas or leisure facilities that offer an array of soothing treatments. For instance, the **Mandarin Oriental Shanghai** offers a signature spa experience that combines traditional Chinese therapies with modern wellness techniques—a perfect way to recharge after your flight. Budget-friendly hotels often provide cozy lounges and local cafes where you can sip on some freshly brewed tea or coffee, a beloved tradition in Shanghai.

If you're feeling energized and keen to start exploring straight away, you can head to the People's Square. Just a short distance from many central hotels, this vast public space in the heart of the city offers a relaxing environment. The green lawns, surrounded by historical buildings and a bustling cityscape, provide a great spot to stretch your legs. Don't forget to check out Shanghai Museum (located right in the square), where you can dive into the city's cultural history with exhibits on ancient Chinese art, calligraphy, and ceramics. The museum's entrance is free, but if you're planning to indulge in a guided tour, expect to pay around ¥60 ($8 USD) per person.

Afternoon: Getting to Know the City's Iconic Spots

By now, you've had some time to relax, but now it's time to get to know Shanghai on a deeper level. One of the best ways to do this is to start with its most famous landmarks, and there's no better place to begin than with the **Bund**. Just a short taxi ride from People's Square or the French Concession, the Bund is Shanghai's most iconic waterfront promenade. Stretching over 1.5 kilometers along the Huangpu River, it's a fascinating fusion of Shanghai's colonial past and its ultramodern present.

As you stroll along the Bund, you'll be surrounded by an impressive row of neoclassical and art-deco buildings, which were once home to foreign banks, consulates, and trading houses during the colonial era. Look across the river at the stunning skyline of **Pudong**, where the futuristic Shanghai Tower, the Oriental Pearl Tower, and the Jin Mao Tower** rise up dramatically from the skyline. This contrast of old and new makes the Bund one of the most picturesque spots in the city. The area is bustling with tourists and locals alike, so take your time to enjoy the views, snap a few photos, and feel the pulse of the city.

If you're into history, make sure to stop by the **Bund History Museum,** located at the southern end of the promenade near Wharves Park. The museum offers a fascinating look at the history of the Bund, Shanghai's rise as a global trading hub, and the architectural styles that adorn the waterfront. Entry is free, though donations are appreciated, and the museum is open daily from 9:30 AM to 5:00 PM.

As the weather starts to warm up, consider enjoying lunch at one of the many restaurants along the Bund. If you're in the mood for something upscale, head to The House of Roosevelt, where you can dine with a view of the river. For a more relaxed atmosphere, check out M on the Bund, a stylish European bistro offering stunning views of the skyline. Expect to spend around ¥150-300 ($20-40 USD) per person for lunch in one of these restaurants.

Evening: A Stroll Along the Bund and Riverfront Views

After your afternoon of exploration, take some time to rest back at your hotel, freshen up, and get ready for an unforgettable evening. The *Bund* takes on a magical quality after sundown. As dusk falls, the iconic buildings along the riverfront begin to light up, and the city's skyline becomes a stunning sea of colors. The shimmering lights of Pudong's skyline, reflecting off the river's surface, create a breathtaking scene, perfect for an evening stroll.

During this time, the Bund is less crowded than during the day, and you can enjoy a peaceful walk along the promenade, soaking in the evening air and admiring the lights of the city. For those who love photography, the Bund offers some of the best

vantage points for capturing Shanghai's skyline. If you're lucky enough to visit on a clear evening, you'll be able to witness one of the most beautiful sunsets in the world, with the sky turning shades of pink and orange, perfectly complementing the architectural beauty of the area.

If you're not too tired and want to explore the Bund's nightlife, consider visiting one of the rooftop bars overlooking the river. The Bar at the *Waldorf Astoria*, located in the opulent Waldorf Astoria Shanghai on the Bund**, is an ideal spot for a cocktail with a view. Another great option is Cloud 9 Bar, situated on the 87th floor of the Jin Mao Tower, which offers a panoramic view of the city's skyline as well as the Huangpu River. Drinks at these bars can be pricey, ranging from ¥80-150 ($10-20 USD) per drink, but the atmosphere and the stunning views make it worth the splurge.

If you're not in the mood for a drink but still want to experience the Bund's enchanting vibe, why not enjoy a river cruise? You can take a Huangpu River Cruise, which is especially popular in the evening when the city's lights are at their brightest. A 1-hour cruise typically costs around ¥70-100 ($10-14 USD) and offers a relaxing way to see the city from a different perspective. Various boats leave from the Bund, with cruises running every 30 minutes from 5:30 PM until late. This is an excellent way to cap off your first day, with the cool breeze of the river and the twinkling lights of Shanghai as your backdrop.

Day 2: Historic Shanghai

Morning: Yuyuan Garden and Old Town Exploration

Start your day with a peaceful visit to *Yuyuan Garden*, one of Shanghai's most famous historical landmarks. Located in the heart of the Old Town, Yuyuan Garden is a classic example of a traditional Chinese garden, complete with elegant pavilions, winding paths, koi-filled ponds, and ancient rock formations. The garden was originally built in the Ming Dynasty by a wealthy official named Pan Yunduan, who sought to create a tranquil retreat for his parents. As you walk through its lush green spaces, you'll find a perfect blend of natural beauty and intricate architecture.

The garden's main entrance is located at 218 Anren Street, and the first thing you'll notice is the grand dragon gate, intricately designed with a golden dragon motif. After passing through the gate, you'll be transported into a world of classical Chinese landscaping, where you can wander through the pavilions, admire the colorful koi fish in the pond, and marvel at the delicate rockeries. The Exquisite Jade Rock, a rare piece of porous rock, is one of the garden's most famous features and is believed to bring good luck to visitors.

The admission fee for Yuyuan Garden is ¥40 ($6 USD) per person, though it's worth noting that there is a combined ticket that also grants access to the Yuyuan Bazaar, a sprawling market area filled with shops and local snacks. The combined ticket costs ¥60 ($9 USD). If you want to skip the long lines at the entrance, you can book your tickets in advance on various online platforms or through your hotel concierge. The garden is typically open from 8:45 AM to 4:45 PM, but it's best to arrive early to avoid the crowds.

After exploring the serene garden, take a stroll through Old Town Shanghai. This area, with its narrow lanes and traditional Chinese architecture, offers a fascinating glimpse into the city's past. As you wander through the

Yuyuan Bazaar, you'll be surrounded by old-style Chinese buildings with ornate wooden facades and decorative rooflines. The bazaar is a great place to pick up souvenirs such as traditional tea sets, silk scarves, and intricate handicrafts. You can also indulge in some of Shanghai's famous street food, such as xiaolongbao (soup dumplings), shengjianbao (pan-fried dumplings), or chive-filled pancakes. Be prepared to pay around ¥10-20 ($2-3 USD) for a small snack from a street vendor.

While in *Old Town*, make sure to stop by Chenghuang Miao, also known as the City God Temple, a stunning Taoist temple dating back to the 14th century. Located just a few minutes from the Yuyuan Garden, the temple offers a glimpse into Shanghai's spiritual heritage. The intricate carvings, wooden beams, and red lanterns create a peaceful atmosphere, perfect for reflection. The temple is free to visit, though donations are encouraged.

Afternoon: Continue Your Journey Through Historic Shanghai

Head over to the *Shanghai Museum*, located in People's Square. This world-class museum is home to an extensive collection of Chinese art, including ancient jade, ceramics, paintings, and calligraphy. The building itself is a masterpiece, designed in the shape of a traditional Chinese cooking vessel, the ding**, symbolizing the fusion of ancient Chinese culture with modern architecture.

The Shanghai Museum is one of the best places to learn about the history of Shanghai and China, and entry is free of charge. It's open daily from 9:00 AM to 5:00 PM (closed on Mondays). Spend a couple of hours here as you wander through the different galleries, each highlighting a different period or aspect of Chinese art and culture. Highlights include the Ancient Chinese Bronze Gallery, the Chinese Painting Galler, and the Jade Gallery, where you can get a closer look at delicate pieces of jade craftsmanship dating back over 3,000 years.

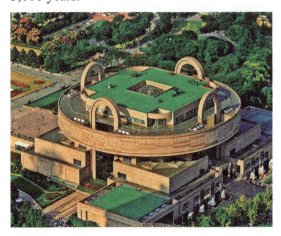

For lunch, step out of the museum and into the People's Square area, which is teeming with options. You could head to Xintiandi, a fashionable area filled with restaurants, cafes, and shops housed in restored traditional shikumen buildings. Here you'll find everything from upscale international fare to delicious local Shanghainese dishes. Try the shanghai-style noodles or a bowl of hot wonton soup perfectly comforting for the rainy or cool afternoons. A typical lunch in this area can cost around ¥50-100 ($7-14 USD) depending on where you eat.

Another great option is to explore Huaihai Road, a popular shopping street that has a mix of international brands and local shops. If you're in the mood for a more relaxed meal, grab a quick bite at one of the many small eateries serving **baozi** (steamed buns) or jianbing (Chinese pancakes). These are inexpensive snacks, usually costing ¥15-30 ($2-4 USD).

Evening: Evening River Cruise

By the time evening rolls around, it's time to unwind and take in the iconic sights of Shanghai from a different perspective—a river cruise. This is the perfect way to wrap up your day, especially after an afternoon spent exploring the historic side of Shanghai. The **Huangpu River Cruise** is one of the best ways to see the city's skyline, as it takes you down the river, offering views of both the old colonial architecture of the Bund and the ultra-modern skyscrapers of Pudong.

Most river cruises depart from Shiliupu Dock, located near the southern tip of the Bund. You can easily reach the dock by walking or taking a short taxi ride from the People's Square area. The Huangpu River Cruise is available in both daytime and evening options, but the evening cruise is particularly spectacular. As night falls, the skyscrapers in Pudong, like the Shanghai Tower and the Oriental Pearl Tower, light up in vibrant colors, offering a view of the city that is truly mesmerizing.

The evening cruise typically lasts about 1 hour and costs between ¥70-150 ($10-20 USD) depending on the type of boat and seating class. The boats usually operate from 5:30 PM to 9:30 PM, but it's best to check the schedule and book your tickets in advance, especially during peak tourist seasons. You can easily book your tickets online or directly at the dock. During the cruise, you'll glide past some of Shanghai's most famous landmarks, including the Waibaidu Bridge and The Bund**, and catch glimpses of the historic waterfront buildings that have witnessed Shanghai's evolution over the years.

While on the boat, take the time to enjoy the cool evening breeze, snap some stunning photos, and reflect on the day. The shimmering skyline, the illuminated buildings, and the peaceful flow of the river make this experience unforgettable. It's a moment to relax, soak in the city's energy, and appreciate how Shanghai blends old-world charm with futuristic ambition.

Day 3: Modern Marvels

Morning: Shanghai Tower – Soaring to New Heights

Your day begins with an exhilarating visit to the **Shanghai Tower**, currently the tallest building in China and the second tallest in the world. Located in the heart of the Lujiazui Financial District in Pudong, the Shanghai Tower offers a breathtaking view of the city from its observation deck on the 118th floor. You can reach the tower by taking the Metro Line 2 to Lujiazui Station and following the signs to the tower. The tower is located at 501 Yincheng Middle Road, a mere five-minute walk from the station.

As you approach the building, you can't help but be impressed by its sleek, twisting design that reaches a height of 632 meters (2,073 feet). Designed by architect Gensler, the building is a marvel of engineering, built to withstand extreme weather and seismic activity. Once inside, make your way to the Shanghai Tower Observation Deck, where you'll be greeted by panoramic views of the city skyline, the iconic Bund, and the nearby Pudong area, including the Shanghai World Financial Center and the Jin Mao Tower. The views from here are absolutely spectacular, especially on a clear day.

To reach the observation deck, you'll take a high-speed elevator that whisks you up in just 55 seconds. Once at the top, you can step onto the glass-floored Sky Walk for an added thrill, looking straight down at the city below. The 360-degree views offer a completely new perspective on Shanghai, allowing you to see the contrasts between its modern skyscrapers and historic districts.

Ticket prices for the Shanghai Tower observation deck vary: ¥180 ($25 USD) for adults, ¥90 ($12 USD) for children, and seniors. The tower is open from 8:30 AM to 9:00 PM, and it's advisable to visit early in the day to avoid the crowds, especially on weekends. If you're planning on visiting other nearby attractions, consider purchasing a combo ticket for the Shanghai Tower, which can save you money if you plan to visit the Oriental Pearl Tower later in the day.

Afternoon: Oriental Pearl TV Tower – Another Icon of Shanghai's Skyline

After your sky-high experience at the Shanghai Tower, it's time to visit one of the city's most recognizable landmarks—the **Oriental Pearl TV Tower.** Located on the banks of the Huangpu River, just a short 15-minute walk from the Shanghai Tower, this iconic structure stands at 468 meters (1,535 feet) tall, making it the third tallest TV tower in the world. Built in 1994, the tower has become synonymous with Shanghai's skyline, thanks to its unique design featuring multiple spherical levels stacked on top of each other.

You can reach the tower by walking to Pudong's Lujiazui area and heading to Hongkou District, where the tower's entrance is located at 1 Century Avenue, Shanghai. The Oriental Pearl Tower is easily accessible by both metro (Line 2) and taxi.

Once you arrive at the tower, purchase your tickets at the main entrance. A single ticket for the observation deck costs ¥160 ($22 USD), though if you want to visit other attractions inside the tower, such as the glass-bottomed viewing platform or the Shanghai History Museum, there are combo tickets available starting from ¥220 ($30 USD).

The tower's observation deck offers incredible views of Pudong and the Bund, but what makes this tower particularly special is the Glass Floor on the 259-meter-high level. The view from the glass floor is truly exhilarating, as you can look straight down at the bustling streets below. Be prepared for a heart-racing experience if you're not a fan of heights!

Apart from the observation decks, the tower houses the Shanghai History Museum, where you can explore exhibitions about the city's past, from its early colonial days to its rapid development into a global metropolis. If you're interested in learning about Shanghai's fascinating transformation, this museum is a must-see. Admission to the museum is typically included with the observation deck ticket.

If you're not yet feeling saturated with breathtaking views, make sure to stop by the **Revolving Restaurant** at the top of the tower. This restaurant slowly rotates, offering a 360-degree panoramic view of Shanghai as you dine. While a meal here can be expensive, it's worth the experience for both the views and the unique setting.

Late Afternoon: Shopping on Nanjing Road

After taking in two of Shanghai's most famous skyscrapers, it's time to indulge in some retail therapy on Nanjing Road, one of the busiest shopping streets in the world. Nanjing Road stretches from **The Bund** to People's Square, a distance of about 5 kilometers (3 miles). It is split into two main sections: East Nanjing Road, which is home to many high-end shopping malls, and **West Nanjing Road, which has a mix of local boutiques and department stores.

To get there from the Oriental Pearl Tower, simply take Metro Line 2 from the Lujiazui Station to Nanjing Road East Station. Alternatively, you can walk or take a quick taxi ride.

Nanjing Road is a shopper's paradise, and whether you're looking for luxury brands, local fashion, or traditional Chinese souvenirs, you'll find something to suit your style and budget. High-end malls like the Plaza 66, Shanghai Times Square, and Super Brand Mall** offer international brands like Louis Vuitton, Gucci, and Apple. Expect to pay a premium for these luxury goods, with prices ranging from ¥1,000-10,000 ($140-1,400 USD) depending on the item.

For a more affordable shopping experience, head to West Nanjing Road, where you can explore department stores such as **Shin Kong Place and Jing An Kerry Centre. You'll find a wide range of goods, from trendy clothes and accessories to household items and electronics, with prices averaging ¥200-1,500 ($30-210 USD) depending on the store and item.

For those looking to pick up unique, locally crafted souvenirs, visit one of the many street vendors that line the road, offering items like traditional Chinese teas, hand-painted silk scarves, and intricate handicrafts. A small souvenir like a Chinese tea set can cost around ¥100-300 ($14-40 USD).

As evening approaches, the street lights of Nanjing Road create a dazzling spectacle, making it the perfect time to explore the area.

Take your time to wander, people-watch, and perhaps grab a bite to eat at one of the many restaurants along the way. Nanjing Road is lined with eateries offering everything from traditional Shanghai-style dim sum to international cuisine, with prices ranging from ¥50-200 ($7-30 USD) for a meal, depending on your choice of restaurant.

Evening: Dining and Exploring the Bund at Night

Finish your day with a visit to The Bund, a riverside promenade that offers spectacular views of Shanghai's skyline. The area is especially magical at night, when the buildings along the river are lit up in a stunning array of colors. This is the perfect place to relax, enjoy a drink, and take in the dazzling lights of the **Pudong skyline**. There are plenty of bars and restaurants lining the Bund where you can enjoy a meal with a view.

Day 4: Cultural Immersion

Morning: Longhua Temple – A Peaceful Retreat

Longhua Temple, located at 2853 Longhua Road, in the Xuhui District. The easiest way to get there from People's Square is by taking Metro Line 1 from People's Square Station** towards Xinzhuang**, and alighting at Longhua Station. From there, it's just a short 10-minute walk to the temple.

The Longhua Temple, originally built during the Three Kingdoms Period (circa 242 AD), is the oldest and largest Buddhist temple in Shanghai, making it a must-visit for anyone interested in Shanghai's religious and cultural history. The temple complex is famous for its ancient architecture, peaceful gardens, and the Longhua Pagoda, which stands at 40 meters (131 feet) and is one of Shanghai's tallest and oldest pagodas. The temple is a stunning example of traditional Chinese Buddhist architecture, with intricate wood carvings, colorful murals, and statues of Buddha.

One of the most unique aspects of Longhua Temple is the sound of the giant bell, which is struck every morning and evening, adding an atmosphere of tranquility. You may want to visit during one of these times for a truly immersive experience. Inside the temple, you'll find several halls, each dedicated to different Buddhist deities. The Daxiong Baodian (Hall of Great Hero) houses a large, golden statue of the Buddha, while the

Guanyin Hall is dedicated to the Goddess of Mercy.

To make your visit even more memorable, participate in a Buddhist prayer ceremony. Visitors are welcome to light incense and offer prayers at the temple's various altars. The temple also has a small Buddhist shop where you can purchase souvenirs such as prayer beads, incense, and statues of Buddha. Admission is ¥10 ($1.50 USD), and the temple is open from 7:00 AM to 5:00 PM. Allow 1-1.5 hours for your visit, as it's a serene and peaceful experience where you can take time to reflect and immerse yourself in the Buddhist culture of Shanghai.

Late Afternoon: The Former French Concession – A Walk Through History

Former French Concession. This area, with its tree-lined streets, colonial architecture, and fashionable boutiques, provides a stark contrast to the modern skyscrapers of Pudong or the bustle of Nanjing Road. The **Former French Concession** refers to the area that was once under French control in the 19th and early 20th centuries, and its European influences are still visible today in the streets and buildings.

To get there from Longhua Temple, take Metro Line 7 at Longhua Station, transfer at Xujiahui Station to Line 1, and alight at Hengshan Road Station. From here, it's a short walk to the heart of the Former French Concession. You can also take a taxi if you prefer a more direct route.

Start your exploration at Tianzifang, a quaint art village tucked away in a maze of narrow alleys. This area, located near Tai Kang Road, is home to a vibrant collection of art galleries, artisan shops, coffee shops, and boutiques. It's a fantastic place to pick up unique souvenirs, such as hand-painted ceramics, custom jewelry, or locally made silk scarves. The area is also filled with charming cafes, perfect for taking a break with a cup of coffee or tea while soaking in the local atmosphere.

Stroll along Fuxing Road, where you'll find beautiful old villas, leafy parks, and stylish boutiques housed in restored French-style buildings. The neighborhood has a laid-back European feel, with cafes spilling out onto the sidewalks, and it's a favorite spot for locals and expats alike. Stop by the Sinan Mansions, a well-preserved group of early 20th-century European-style buildings, or wander through the Xintiandi area, known for its blend of old Shanghai architecture and modern luxury.

If you enjoy browsing historical buildings, you can visit the Shanghai Propaganda Poster Art Centre on Dongtai Road. This museum showcases a fascinating collection of Chinese propaganda posters from the **Cultural Revolution** period, offering a unique perspective on China's history. The entrance fee is ¥30 ($4 USD).

After exploring the district's historical charm, indulge in a delicious dinner at one of the many trendy restaurants in the area. Xintiandi offers a variety of dining options, ranging from traditional Chinese cuisine to international flavors, and many restaurants offer al fresco dining, allowing you to enjoy the vibrant street scene. A typical dinner here can cost anywhere from ¥100-300 ($15-$40 USD), depending on the venue.

Evening: Relaxing in the Former French Concession

After your exploration, take some time to relax and enjoy the atmosphere of the Former French Concession. It's the perfect spot to unwind after a busy day of sightseeing. You can enjoy an evening cocktail at one of the many stylish bars in the area, such as The House of Roosevelt, which offers both excellent drinks and great views of the city, or head to one of the laid-back cafes for a relaxing end to your cultural journey.

Day 5: Outdoor Adventures

Morning: Relax in Century Park

Start your day with a visit to **Century Park**, located in the Pudong New Area, at 1001 Jinxiu Road, just north of the Lujiazui financial district. This vast park, covering 140 hectares (350 acres), is Shanghai's largest and most well-known urban park, offering a peaceful oasis away from the city's hustle and bustle. To get there, simply take Metro Line 2 and alight at Century Park Station, which is just a short walk from the park entrance.

Century Park is an ideal spot for a relaxing morning, with its expansive green lawns, tranquil lakes, and winding paths. The park features a blend of traditional Chinese landscaping and modern design elements, including lush flower beds, man-made lakes, and several themed gardens. It's the perfect place to start the day by strolling under towering trees, enjoying the fresh air, or simply relaxing on the grass with a good book.

One of the park's most beautiful spots is the Century Park Lake, a 15-hectare water feature that is home to swans, ducks, and other waterfowl. If you're in the mood for a bit of light exercise, you can rent a pedal boat or a rowboat to paddle on the lake, which costs around ¥40-60 ($6-$9 USD) for an hour of fun. Alternatively, if you're looking for something even more peaceful, head to the Chinese Garden within the park. It's designed with classical elements such as rockeries, ponds, and bamboo groves, offering a quiet place to reflect and unwind.

For those interested in art and culture, the Century Park Museum located within the park is also worth a visit. The museum features rotating exhibitions that highlight both Chinese and international art, offering a more cultural experience in the midst of nature. Admission to the museum is typically ¥30 ($4 USD), though prices can vary depending on the exhibits.

If you prefer something more active, Century Park also features cycling tracks, rollerblading paths, and outdoor fitness equipment scattered throughout the park. You can rent a bike for around ¥40 ($6 USD) for an hour, which is a fun way to explore the park's extensive paths and see the many scenic areas, including the Lakeside Scenic Area and the Botanical Garden.

You'll want to spend at least 2-3 hours here, enjoying the fresh air, the natural beauty, and the variety of activities on offer. If you get hungry, there are several cafes and snack bars around the park that serve light refreshments, perfect for a morning break.

Afternoon: Huangpu River Activities

After enjoying the serenity of Century Park, head over to the Huangpu River, which flows through the heart of Shanghai and offers countless opportunities for outdoor activities. The Huangpu River, which separates the city into two parts – the historic Puxi and the modern Pudong districts – is not just a landmark; it's an essential part of the city's life, with a waterfront filled with attractions and activities.

To get to the river, take Metro Line 2 from Century Park Station to **Lujiazui Station** (about 10 minutes). From there, head towards the riverfront area, where you'll find various piers and promenades along the water.

One of the best ways to experience the Huangpu River is by taking a river cruise. Shanghai offers a range of cruise options, both during the day and at night. For a daytime experience, board one of the classic Huangpu River Cruises, which typically depart from the Shiliupu Pier or the Pudong Riverside Promenade. These cruises offer a leisurely 1-hour journey along the river, where you can enjoy panoramic views of the city's iconic skyline, including the Bund, the Pudong skyscrapers, and Lujiazui's futuristic architecture. The river cruise provides a unique perspective of Shanghai's history and modernity, as the Bund represents Shanghai's colonial past, while Pudong's skyscrapers showcase its rise as a global financial hub.

Ticket prices for a daytime river cruise generally range from ¥70-150 ($10-$21 USD) depending on the type of boat and the level of service. It's a great way to rest and take in the sights. If you prefer a more private experience, you can book a luxury yacht** or private boat rental, which costs around ¥600-1000 ($85-$140 USD) per hour, depending on the boat.

For those looking for more adventure, there are a number of water sports activities available on the Huangpu River. You can try your hand at kayaking, stand-up paddleboarding (SUP), or even jet skiing**. These activities are popular during the warmer months and are offered by various companies operating along the riverfront. Prices for these activities vary, but a 30-minute kayaking session or SUP rental typically costs around ¥100-200 ($14-$28 USD), making it an

exciting way to get up close to the river while enjoying some physical activity.

If you're in the mood for a relaxing riverside walk, the Riverside Promenade (also known as Binjiang Avenue) is a lovely place to stroll along the river. Stretching from Pudong to The Bund, this pedestrian-friendly promenade offers fantastic views of Shanghai's skyline and is ideal for a peaceful afternoon walk. It's a great spot to take photos, watch the boats pass by, or simply enjoy the city's energy as it comes to life along the water.

Evening: Huangpu River by Night

As the day winds down, the Huangpu River transforms into a dazzling spectacle of lights, making it one of the most iconic views in Shanghai. To get the best experience, consider taking an evening river cruise, where you'll have the chance to see the Pudong skyline and The Bund lit up in all their glory. The city's modern skyscrapers, including the Shanghai Tower and Oriental Pearl TV Tower, are beautifully illuminated, offering a truly breathtaking scene.

Evening cruises typically depart around 7:00 PM to 8:00 PM, and they are a must-do for anyone visiting Shanghai. The price for a nighttime river cruise ranges from ¥120-250 ($17-$35 USD), depending on the type of cruise. If you want to make the experience even more special, consider booking a private boat** with dinner or drinks included. This is the perfect way to cap off a day of outdoor adventures, with the city's glowing skyline as your backdrop.

Alternatively, if you'd rather enjoy the river views from the shore, there are numerous bars and restaurants along the Bund that offer rooftop dining and cocktails with a view. Many of these venues offer stunning views of the river, and you can watch the lights come on as the city transforms into a luminous wonderland. Expect to pay around ¥100-300 ($14-$42 USD) per person for a cocktail or light dinner, depending on the venue.

Day 6: Day Trip to a Water Town

Morning: Journey to Zhujiajiao

Begin your day early, aiming to leave Shanghai by 8:00 AM so that you can maximize your time in the water town. There are several ways to get to Zhujiajiao, one of

Shanghai's closest water towns, located about 45 minutes (45 km) from the city center. You can take a private taxi, which will cost around ¥200-300 ($30-$42 USD) one way, or take public transportation, which is more economical. To reach Zhujiajiao by metro, take Line 17 from Shanghai South Railway Station to Zhujiajiao Station, and from there, it's a short walk to the town's main attractions.

Zhujiajiao is one of the most well-preserved ancient water towns in the region, dating back over 1,700 years. Upon arrival, you'll be greeted by narrow, winding streets, traditional stone bridges, and ancient white-washed houses that line the canals. The town, often referred to as "Shanghai's Venice," is dotted with small shops, teahouses, and artisanal stalls that sell local crafts and snacks.

The town is famous for its quaint canals and traditional wooden boats, which you can take for a relaxing ride. A boat ride on the canals costs around ¥40-80 ($6-$11 USD) per person, depending on the duration. You'll glide under stone bridges, passing by charming traditional homes and lush greenery.

During the ride, you'll get a great view of Zhujiajiao's peaceful riverside life, where residents continue their centuries-old traditions. A boat ride here is both scenic and a great way to get a sense of local life.

After your boat ride, take some time to stroll through the narrow streets of the town. Visit Kezhi Garden, one of the most famous historical attractions in Zhujiajiao. This traditional Chinese garden is over 400 years old and features beautiful pavilions, ponds, and rockeries. Entrance to the garden costs about ¥30 ($4 USD). It's a great place to take a walk and enjoy the tranquility of the town.

As you wander through Zhujiajiao, stop for a bite at one of the local eateries serving shrimps in a rich ginger sauce** or the town's specialty, Zhujiajiao rice cakes. These local delicacies are a must-try and will give you a taste of the traditional cuisine of the water towns. A meal here typically costs around ¥30-60 ($4-$8 USD) per person.

Afternoon: Explore Suzhou's Classical Gardens

Alternatively, if you decide to visit Suzhou, a city that is 1.5 to 2 hours by train from Shanghai, you will be introduced to its famed classical gardens, silk culture, and ancient architecture. Suzhou is a UNESCO World Heritage site, renowned for its garden designs, which date back to the 11th century. You can take a high-speed train from Shanghai Railway Station to Suzhou, which takes about 30 minutes, or opt for a private taxi for a more leisurely and comfortable trip, which would cost around ¥400-500 ($56-$70 USD) one way.

Upon arrival in Suzhou, head straight to one of the city's classical gardens he most famous being the Humble Administrator's Garden (Zhuo Zheng Yuan). Known for its beautiful ponds, pavilions, and bamboo groves, the garden is a symbol of classical Chinese landscaping. Entry costs around ¥70 ($10 USD). Spend a couple of hours meandering through this tranquil garden, appreciating its delicate design and peaceful atmosphere. Afterward, head to the Lingering Garden or the Master of Nets Garden both are stunning examples of Suzhou's garden design and worth a visit if you have the time.

You'll also want to stop by Pingjiang Road, an ancient street lined with traditional houses, tea shops, and silk boutiques. This area has the charm of an ancient town but with the vibrancy of a modern city. You can browse the silk markets, as Suzhou is famous for its silk production. Don't miss the chance to pick up a silk scarf or a piece of embroidered artwork as a unique souvenir.

For lunch, try a local Suzhou delicacy, Suan La Tang (hot and sour soup), which is a perfect dish to energize you for the afternoon. A typical meal at a local restaurant in Suzhou costs around ¥50-80 ($7-$11 USD) per person.

Evening: Return to Shanghai for Dinner

After a full day of exploring Zhujiajiao or Suzhou, it's time to head back to Shanghai. If you've been to Zhujiajiao, you can take a taxi or*Metro Line 17 to return to the city in about 45 minutes. If you've visited Suzhou, take the high-speed train back to Shanghai, which will take around 30 minutes.

Once back in Shanghai, you'll be ready to enjoy a delicious dinner at one of the city's many excellent restaurants. Depending on your mood and location, you have several options for a fantastic meal. If you're looking for something upscale and cosmopolitan, head to the Bund, where you can dine with a stunning view of the skyline and the Huangpu River. M on the Bund, a famous restaurant, offers international and fusion cuisine with spectacular views. A meal here will cost around ¥200-400 ($28-$56 USD) per person, depending on your selection.

If you'd prefer something more casual but equally delicious, Jia Jia Tang Bao, located near People's Square, is a famous spot for Xiaolongbao (soup dumplings) and other Shanghai-style dishes. It's one of the most beloved spots for both locals and tourists, and a meal here typically costs around ¥50-80 ($7-$11 USD).

For a relaxing evening, consider a quiet meal in the French Concession area, which is filled with charming bistros and cafes. The Commune Social is a popular choice, offering a unique twist on contemporary Chinese food in a chic, modern setting. Expect to spend around ¥150-300 ($21-$42 USD) for dinner.

After your meal, take a leisurely stroll along the Bund, where you can appreciate the dazzling night lights of Shanghai's skyline. Alternatively, if you're feeling adventurous, check out one of the local jazz bars or rooftop lounges for a nightcap. The Jazz Bar at the Peace Hotel is a great place to unwind with a classic cocktail and live music. Entrance fees may vary, but a drink typically costs ¥80-150 ($11-$21 USD)

Day 7: Farewell to Shanghai

Morning: Final Shopping in Shanghai

Start your final day with a relaxed morning of shopping, an activity that blends perfectly with Shanghai's chic urban vibe. Head to Nanjing Road, Shanghai's famous shopping street, for your last chance to pick up souvenirs or luxury items. Whether you're looking for designer goods, local crafts, or unique keepsakes, this iconic street offers an eclectic mix of shops to suit every taste and budget. Located in the heart of the city, Nanjing Road East is easily accessible via the People's Square Metro Station (Lines 1, 2, and 8), and you can spend a few hours here strolling along the wide pedestrian avenue.

For a more high-end shopping experience, make sure to stop by Plaza 66, one of Shanghai's premier luxury malls, located at 1266 Nanjing West Road. This mall boasts a range of international luxury brands like Louis Vuitton, Gucci, and Chanel, offering the perfect opportunity to splurge or simply enjoy window shopping. Shopping here will cost you as much or as little as you like, with some high-end items starting from ¥5,000 ($700 USD), while smaller purchases, like accessories or perfume, may range from ¥500-2,000 ($70-$280 USD).

If you're interested in something more unique, Tianzifang, located in the French Concession area, is a great alternative for artisanal products and handicrafts. Wander through the narrow lanes and discover handcrafted jewelry, vintage clothing, and one-of-a-kind souvenirs. The old, charming buildings have been converted into a maze of boutiques, galleries, and cafés. It's also a perfect spot to pick up a unique piece of Shanghai's creative energy, from art prints to handmade soaps. A visit here is more about the experience of browsing and enjoying the local craftsmanship than the actual price tags, with most items ranging from ¥50-500 ($7-$70 USD).

By mid-morning, you may feel the need for a little respite before your next activity, and The Bund is a perfect spot for a quick coffee break. Take a seat at one of the cafés with a view of the river, like Café de la Poste in the Bund 18 Building. Here, you can sip a cappuccino while soaking in the majestic view of Shanghai's skyline, a beautiful contrast of old European-style buildings with the towering skyscrapers of Pudong.

Afternoon: Traditional Chinese Tea Ceremony Experience

No visit to Shanghai is complete without experiencing a traditional Chinese tea ceremony, and this afternoon will offer the perfect opportunity to immerse yourself in this cultural practice. The tea ceremony is an integral part of Chinese culture, a meditative ritual that emphasizes respect, mindfulness, and appreciation for nature. Shanghai is home to several renowned tea houses where you can partake in this tranquil experience, and the Wuyi Tea House located in Tianzifang is one of the best.

To get there, simply take a short 15-minute wall from the shopping area, and you'll be immersed in a peaceful haven of quiet contemplation. The tea house offers several tea-tasting experiences, ranging from green tea to the more complex Pu-erh tea. A tea ceremony usually lasts around 45 minutes to an hour, and the expert tea master will guide you through the entire process— explaining the history and nuances of the tea leaves, as well as the proper techniques for brewing and savoring the tea. Expect to pay about ¥100-200 ($14-$28 USD) per person for a full tea ceremony, which includes a selection of teas and traditional snacks like sweet rice cakes and sesame pastries.

After the ceremony, you may want to browse the shop for some tea to take home. This is a great way to remember your time in Shanghai, and you can find high-quality teas at various price points. A loose-leaf tea package can range from ¥50-300 ($7-$42 USD)**, depending on the variety and packaging.

Alternatively, if you're short on time or prefer a more convenient option, Teakha in Huangpu District is another excellent tea house, offering a wide selection of premium teas served in a relaxed atmosphere. Located at 14 Sinan Road, it's known for its cozy ambiance and knowledgeable staff, making it a perfect stop for tea lovers looking for a quieter experience.

Evening: Departure Preparations and Final Reflections

As the afternoon draws to a close, it's time to start preparing for your departure from Shanghai. Depending on your flight time, plan to leave for the airport about 2-3 hours before your departur*. Shanghai is served by two airports: Shanghai Pudong International Airport (PVG) and Shanghai Hongqiao International Airport (SHA). Most international flights depart from Pudong, while Hongqiao mainly handles domestic flights.

If you're traveling from Pudong Airport, take the Maglev train from Longyang Road Station, which connects you to the airport in just 8 minutes. Alternatively, a taxi will cost around ¥150-200 ($21-$28 USD) and take 40-60 minutes depending on traffic. If you're flying from Hongqiao Airport, the Metro Line 2 is a quick and affordable option, taking **30 minutes to reach the airport for around ¥5-10 ($0.70-$1.40 USD).

Before leaving, take a moment to reflect on your time in Shanghai. Whether you've enjoyed the majestic skyscrapers of the city center, marveled at the ancient temples, explored the gardens and canals, or indulged in delicious local food, Shanghai's unique mix of modernity and tradition leaves a lasting impression. This city is constantly evolving, and each visit offers new discoveries.Once you arrive at the airport, be sure to allow time for the check-in process, especially if you are traveling during peak hours. Make sure your luggage complies with airport regulations, and don't forget to check for any duty-free shopping, where you can find luxury goods like cosmetics, jewelry, and even souvenirs to bring home.

As your flight departs, gaze out the window and say a final goodbye to Shanghai's sparkling skyline, knowing that the memories you've made here will last a lifetime. Whether you plan to return someday or simply carry the experiences with you, Shanghai will always remain an unforgettable destination— where the old meets the new, where traditions are cherished, and where a future of infinite possibilities continues to unfold.

PRACTICAL INFORMATION AND TIPS

Transportation in Shanghai

Metro System: Key Lines and Stops for Tourists

The Shanghai Metro is undoubtedly one of the fastest and most convenient ways to get around the city. With 14 lines and over 400 stations, it covers the entirety of the city and even extends to suburban areas. The system is incredibly user-friendly, with signs in both Chinese and English, making it easy for tourists to navigate.

Key metro lines that are particularly useful for visitors include:

Line 1 (Red Line): This line is vital for tourists as it connects many of the major attractions in the city. It passes through People's Square (a hub for shopping, museums, and the Shanghai Grand Theatre), the Nanjing Road shopping district, and the Bund, where you can enjoy the famous skyline and the historic architecture of the city.

Line 2 (Green Line): This line runs from Pudong Airport to the western parts of Shanghai and is another key line for tourists. Stops like Lujiazui (the financial district) are on this line, which is perfect if you want to see landmarks such as the Oriental Pearl Tower, Shanghai Tower, and Jin Mao Tower.

Line 10 (Purple Line): This line is handy for visiting Yuyuan Garden and Old Shanghai, as well as getting to Tianzifang, a famous art and craft district.

The metro operates from 5:30 AM to 11:00 PM, with trains arriving every 2-3 minutes during peak hours. A one-way ride typically costs between ¥3-12 ($0.50-$1.70 USD) depending on the distance, and tickets can be purchased at ticket vending machines or the customer service desk. Alternatively, you can get a Shanghai Public Transportation Card, which is a rechargeable smart card that allows you to easily hop on and off buses and the metro.

Taxis, Rideshares, and Bicycles for Getting Around

If you prefer a more direct route or are traveling with luggage, taxis are an excellent choice. Taxis in Shanghai are relatively affordable compared to many other global cities. The base fare is around ¥14 ($2 USD) for the first 3 kilometers, with an additional charge for every kilometer after that. However, it's important to note that traffic congestion can be a problem in certain areas, especially during rush hour, so plan your journey accordingly. Taxis are readily available throughout the city, and you can also book them using apps like Didi, China's equivalent of Uber.

For a more tech-savvy and convenient option, rideshare services like Didi Chuxing offer an easy way to book a ride directly from your smartphone. You can choose from various types of cars, from budget-friendly options to luxury vehicles. The app is available in both Chinese and English, and you can pay for rides via WeChat or Alipay, making it easy for international visitors. The fares are typically similar to that of regular taxis, but the app offers additional convenience by allowing you to book a ride in advance and track your driver in real time.

If you're feeling a bit more adventurous, bicycles and electric scooters are also popular ways to get around. Shanghai has implemented a bike-sharing system, where you can rent bicycles through apps like Mobike and Ofo. These bikes are available at nearly every street corner, and with just a quick scan of a QR code, you can unlock the bike and start your ride. Electric scooters are available through similar platforms and are ideal for short trips. Rental prices start from around ¥1 ($0.14 USD) for a 30-minute ride.

Tips for Navigating Traffic and Crowds

Shanghai is a city known for its fast pace and heavy traffic, especially during rush hours (7:30 AM - 9:30 AM and 5:00 PM - 7:00 PM). If you're planning to use taxis or rideshare services during these times, be prepared for longer travel times. The Metro is often the fastest and most reliable way to get around during these hours, as it avoids the chaos of road traffic. However, crowded metro trains can be an overwhelming experience, particularly on lines such as Line 2, which serve some of the city's busiest stations. Be sure to avoid peak rush hours if possible to have a more comfortable journey.

For tourists unfamiliar with the city, it's recommended to keep the address of your destination written in Chinese (or use a translation app) if you're taking a taxi, as many drivers might not speak English. For bicycles and scooters, always wear a helmet if available, and be aware of local traffic rules. While cycling in Shanghai is generally safe, the roads can be chaotic, and it's essential to keep an eye on both pedestrians and motorized traffic.

Currency and Payments

Using RMB and Popular Payment Apps

The official currency in Shanghai is the Renminbi (RMB), commonly referred to as Chinese Yuan (CNY). The symbol for the yuan is ¥, and banknotes are available in denominations of ¥1, ¥5, ¥10, ¥20, ¥50, and ¥100, while coins are in ¥1, ¥0.5, ¥0.1, and others. While you can certainly use cash for most transactions, Shanghai is a highly digital city where mobile payments dominate. Most locals and businesses use digital payment methods for almost everything, making it convenient for both residents and tourists.

Alipay and WeChat Pay are the two major payment apps in China, and they are widely accepted across Shanghai, from major shopping malls and restaurants to smaller street vendors. These apps are particularly popular due to their speed, convenience, and ability to link directly to your bank account or credit card.

WeChat Pay is part of the WeChat app, which is similar to WhatsApp but with added features like social media, shopping, and payments all in one. Setting it up is straightforward: simply download WeChat, register with your phone number, and link your payment method to the app.

Alipay, owned by Alibaba, functions similarly to WeChat Pay and allows you to scan QR codes for easy transactions. It's also linked to numerous Chinese services, making it highly versatile for both online and in-person payments.

For foreign visitors, both apps offer the ability to link international credit cards (like Visa or MasterCard) to your account, allowing you to use these apps without needing a Chinese bank account. However, setting up these apps can be tricky if you don't speak Chinese, so some tourists prefer to get help from locals or use a translation app to navigate the setup process.

While the apps offer great convenience, cash is still useful, especially in smaller shops or rural areas. Many stores and markets in older districts may not accept digital payments, so it's advisable to carry a small amount of cash for such occasions.

Where to Find Reliable ATMs

If you find yourself in need of cash, there are plenty of ATMs throughout Shanghai. Most international banks, including HSBC, CitiBank, and Bank of China, have ATMs that accept international cards, making it easy for foreign visitors to withdraw cash in RMB. Some of the best places to find these ATMs are:

International Airports: Both Shanghai Pudong International Airport (PVG) and

Shanghai Hongqiao Airport (SHA) have several ATMs that accept foreign cards, especially in the arrival terminals.

Shopping Centers and Malls: Popular malls like Nanjing Road or Shanghai IFC Mall have international ATMs located inside or near the entrances, where you can easily withdraw cash.

Bank Branches: Major banks around the city will have ATMs outside their branches, and you can often find English-speaking staff inside if you need assistance. The Bank of China is particularly reliable for foreign cardholders.

Train Stations and Metro Stations: Key transportation hubs like Shanghai Railway Station and People's Square Metro Station are equipped with ATMs, making them convenient spots to withdraw cash on the go.

It's important to note that ATM fees may apply when withdrawing from foreign accounts, typically ranging from ¥30 to ¥50 ($5-$8 USD) per transaction, plus a conversion fee from your bank. To minimize fees, it's best to withdraw larger sums at once.

Also, while ATMs are generally reliable, be cautious of machines in isolated areas or unlit places. Always ensure the ATM is attached to a reputable bank and has not been tampered with. If in doubt, head to a major bank or a bustling area where you'll find customer service if needed.

Additional Tips for Handling Currency and Payments

Currency Exchange: If you need to exchange foreign currency for RMB, you can do so at banks, currency exchange counters, or airports. However, keep in mind that exchange rates at airports are often less favorable than those found in local banks or exchange offices. China Foreign Exchange and Bank of China offer good rates. Also, it's advisable to bring USD or EUR if you're planning to exchange your currency, as other currencies may not be accepted.

Credit Cards: Most international credit cards like Visa, MasterCard, and American Express are accepted at large hotels, malls, and restaurants in Shanghai. However, in smaller shops, especially in markets or more traditional areas, cash or digital payments via Alipay or WeChat Pay might be your only option. It's a good idea to check with the merchant before committing to a purchase if you plan to pay by card.

Tipping: While tipping is not a common practice in Shanghai, it is appreciated in higher-end restaurants and hotels. In general, tipping is not expected at smaller eateries or for services like taxi rides. Some upscale restaurants may include a service charge in the bill, so be sure to check before leaving an additional tip.

Keep Some Cash Handy: Despite Shanghai's reputation as a cashless society, it's still wise to carry some physical cash, especially if you're planning to visit markets, street food vendors, or traditional neighborhoods. Small businesses and local shops may not have the infrastructure to accept digital payments.

Language and Communication

While its bustling streets are lined with towering skyscrapers, its rich culture is still deeply rooted in its history. For tourists, one of the first things to consider when visiting Shanghai is the language barrier. Mandarin Chinese, also known as Putonghua, is the official language of Shanghai, but the city's unique blend of international influences means that communication can be both exciting and challenging. Here's everything you need to know about language and communication in Shanghai, along with tips to navigate your way through this dynamic metropolis.

Common Mandarin Phrases for Tourists

While many locals in Shanghai understand basic English, especially in tourist-heavy areas, knowing a few essential Mandarin phrases will go a long way in ensuring a smoother experience. Mandarin is the primary language spoken in Shanghai, and the city is predominantly Mandarin-speaking, though Shanghainese, a local dialect, is also widely used by older generations. Understanding some common phrases in Mandarin will not only enhance your experience but also show respect for the local culture.

Here are some key Mandarin phrases every tourist should know:

Hello – 你好 (Nǐ hǎo)

The standard greeting in Mandarin, suitable for almost any situation.

Thank you – 谢谢 (Xièxiè)

A simple and polite way to show gratitude.

Yes – 是的 (Shì de)

A helpful phrase when agreeing or confirming something.

No – 不是 (Bù shì)

For politely declining or negating.

Excuse me – 对不起 (Duìbuqǐ)

A useful phrase when trying to get someone's attention or apologizing.

How much? – 多少钱 (Duōshao qián)

Essential for asking about prices in markets or shops.

Where is...? – ......在哪里? (......zài nǎlǐ?)
Perfect for asking directions (e.g., "Where is the metro station?" 地铁站在哪里?).

I don't understand – 我听不懂 (Wǒ tīng bù dǒng)
When communication breaks down, this phrase can be a lifesaver.

Please – 请 (Qǐng)
Adds politeness to any request.

Goodbye – 再见 (Zàijiàn)
The standard farewell when you're leaving.

Many signs, especially in tourist areas and public transportation hubs, include both Mandarin and English. While the local dialect (Shanghainese) is still used by older generations in informal settings, it's unlikely that tourists will need to learn it, as Mandarin remains the primary language of communication.

English Availability in Tourist Areas

One of the most striking aspects of Shanghai is how international the city feels. Thanks to its status as a global business and tourism hub, English is widely spoken, especially in areas frequented by tourists. In major attractions like The Bund, Yu Garden, Nanjing Road, and Shanghai Disneyland, you'll find signage in both Mandarin and English, making it relatively easy to get around. Many of the staff at international hotels, high-end restaurants, shopping malls, and major attractions speak basic to fluent English, so communication in these areas is generally seamless.

That said, English proficiency can vary depending on the location. In more local neighborhoods, smaller shops, and traditional markets, you may encounter challenges when speaking English. Street vendors, local cafes, and small boutiques often rely on basic Mandarin or Shanghainese, and staff may not speak English. In these cases, learning a few simple phrases, such as asking for help with directions or knowing how to say "thank you" in Mandarin, will be extremely helpful.

In restaurants, especially those catering to tourists or high-end venues, English-speaking staff are quite common. However, in traditional Chinese eateries or lesser-known spots, menus may be in Mandarin or use images instead of text. If you find yourself in a local eatery, apps like Google Translate or Pleco (a Mandarin dictionary app) can help bridge the communication gap, as they allow you to take pictures of the menu and translate text into English instantly.

While not everyone in Shanghai will be fluent in English, the city is increasingly English-friendly, especially in districts like Pudong (home to many international businesses) and Xintiandi (a popular entertainment district). In these neighborhoods, you'll find an abundance of international chain stores, bars, cafes, and restaurants where English is commonly spoken, so you can easily navigate the area without significant language barriers.

Tips for Navigating the Language Barrier

Even though Shanghai is one of China's most international cities, you may still encounter situations where English won't be helpful. Here are some practical tips for navigating language barriers:

Use Translation Apps: Download a translation app like Google Translate, Pleco, or iTranslate on your smartphone. These apps can help you communicate more effectively and translate written or spoken text. Pleco is particularly useful for learning Mandarin phrases and understanding characters.

Learn a Few Key Phrases: As mentioned, learning simple phrases like "Hello," "Thank you," and "How much?" will make interactions more pleasant. Locals will appreciate your effort to speak Mandarin, even if it's just a few words.

Carry a Phrasebook or Offline Dictionary: In case you don't have access to Wi-Fi or data, having a small pocket-sized phrasebook or offline Mandarin dictionary can be a lifesaver. This allows you to ask questions, read menus, or understand signs without worrying about connection issues.

Pointing and Gestures: In case of confusion, pointing at objects, using hand gestures, or showing pictures on your phone (such as a map or a location) can go a long way in helping you communicate. People are usually very patient and willing to help if you show a little effort.

Hotel Concierge and Staff Assistance: If you're staying at an international hotel or a tourist-friendly guesthouse, the concierge and front desk staff can often assist with translation or directions. They may even provide you with printed directions in Mandarin to show taxi drivers or locals.

Look for English Signs and Menus: While not all establishments will have English menus, many tourist-friendly spots will. Look for bilingual signs, and if you're in doubt, it's always a good idea to ask for an English menu.

Health and Safety

For most travelers, the city is an exciting destination, filled with adventure and exploration. However, just as in any major city, it's essential to keep your health and safety in mind while navigating its busy streets and attractions. Here's a practical guide to help you stay safe, including tips for crowded spaces, emergency numbers, and essential hospital information.

Staying Safe in Crowded Spaces

Shanghai is one of the most populous cities in the world, with an estimated population of over 24 million people. Naturally, this means that some of its busiest spots—like Nanjing Road, The Bund, and Yu Garden—can get quite crowded, especially during peak hours, weekends, and holidays. While the energy and vibrancy of these crowds are part of Shanghai's charm, it's important to be mindful of your safety in these bustling environments.

Pickpocketing: In crowded areas, pickpocketing can occasionally be a concern, though it's not widespread. Always keep your valuables secure and avoid carrying large amounts of cash. Use a money belt or neck pouch if possible, and ensure your wallet or phone is safely tucked away in a front pocket or an anti-theft bag. Be cautious when dealing with street vendors or in areas where there are large groups of people, as distractions can sometimes be used to steal.

Traffic Safety: Shanghai's streets are incredibly busy, with a mix of cars, bicycles, scooters, and pedestrians. When crossing streets, always wait for the pedestrian signal, even if traffic seems light. Although many areas have designated pedestrian zones, some areas can still be dangerous for foot traffic due to the fast-paced movement of vehicles and bicycles. Be vigilant, and remember that pedestrians do not always have the right of way, especially in less tourist-heavy areas.

Avoiding Heat Exhaustion: Shanghai has a subtropical climate, with hot and humid summers. During the summer months (June to August), temperatures can rise above 35°C (95°F), which can make outdoor activities uncomfortable. When navigating crowded spaces during this time, be mindful of the risk of heat exhaustion. Stay hydrated, wear sunscreen, and avoid long exposure to the sun during the hottest parts of the day, typically between 11 a.m. and 3 p.m.

Staying Aware in Public Transit: Shanghai's metro system is fast, efficient, and well-connected, but it can also get extremely crowded, especially during rush hours (7-9 a.m. and 5-7 p.m.). When traveling on the metro, be cautious with your personal belongings, as the sheer volume of people can create opportunities for petty theft. Always keep an eye on your bags and stay alert when disembarking or waiting in crowded stations. Also, be prepared for the occasional push or shove—crowded metro trains are a normal part of the Shanghai experience!

Emergency Numbers and Hospitals

While Shanghai is a safe city for travelers, emergencies can still arise. Knowing the right emergency numbers and where to find medical help will give you peace of mind during your stay.

Emergency Numbers:

- Police: 110
- Fire: 119
- Ambulance: 120
- Traffic Accidents: 122

These emergency numbers are available 24/7, and operators generally speak Mandarin. If you do not speak Mandarin, it can be helpful to have your hotel address or a local friend write down your issue in Chinese before you call. For visitors with smartphones, translation apps like Google Translate or Pleco can also help bridge the language gap in an emergency situation.

Hospitals and Medical Care: Shanghai has excellent medical facilities, including international hospitals that cater to the needs of tourists and expatriates. In case of a medical emergency, it's advisable to go to one of the city's well-regarded hospitals, where English-speaking doctors and staff are available.

Top hospitals for tourists:

ParkwayHealth Shanghai (International Hospital)

- Address: 1159 Changning Road, Changning District, Shanghai
- Known for its international standard of healthcare, ParkwayHealth has English-speaking staff and caters to expatriates and tourists. It offers a range of medical services from general consultations to emergency care.
- Phone: +86 21 3212 6600

Jiahui International Hospital

- Address: 1001 Changshou Road, Putuo District, Shanghai
- A modern healthcare facility providing high-quality services to both locals and expatriates. They offer emergency services, general medical care, and specialist consultations.
- Phone: +86 21 2218 5100

Shanghai United Family Hospital

- Address: 1139 Xianxia Road, Changning District, Shanghai
- This hospital is another well-regarded option for international patients. It has an extensive emergency care unit and provides multilingual services, making it accessible to tourists.
- Phone: +86 21 2216 3900

If you need medications, you can easily find pharmacies in major shopping malls and around tourist areas. However, it's always a good idea to carry any prescription medications you may need, along with a note from your doctor detailing your prescription in case of an emergency.

Health Insurance and Travel Insurance

Travel insurance that covers medical emergencies is highly recommended when visiting Shanghai, as healthcare costs can add up quickly, especially if you need to be hospitalized or require specialized care. Ensure that your travel insurance covers emergency medical expenses, as well as emergency evacuation, in case of more serious incidents.

If you are traveling with children or elderly relatives, consider purchasing comprehensive travel insurance that includes coverage for potential medical needs, such as hospitalization or emergency care, as well as any activities you may be engaging in.

Safety Tips for Travelers

Stay Hydrated: In Shanghai's hot and humid summer, it's easy to get dehydrated. Carry a reusable water bottle with you, and refill it at public water fountains or inside cafes and shops.

Respect Local Customs: While Shanghai is a cosmopolitan city, it's always a good idea to be mindful of local customs. For instance, if you're visiting temples or other sacred sites, be respectful of the rules and dress modestly.

Watch for Air Pollution: Shanghai occasionally experiences high levels of air pollution, particularly during the winter months. If you are sensitive to air quality or have respiratory conditions, consider wearing a mask and checking the air quality index before venturing out.

Know Your Nearest Embassy: In the rare event that you lose your passport or face other serious issues, knowing the location of your embassy can be crucial. For U.S. citizens, the U.S. Consulate General Shanghai is located at 1469 Huaihai Zhong Road. For other nationals, check the website of your respective embassy for emergency assistance.

Local Customs and Etiquette

While the city is generally welcoming to visitors from around the world, understanding local customs and etiquette will help you make a positive impression and avoid inadvertently offending anyone. From dining etiquette to cultural do's and don'ts, here's a guide to ensure you navigate Shanghai with respect and understanding.

Dining Etiquette in China

Dining in Shanghai is an experience in itself, rich with flavors, aromas, and a strong sense of tradition. It's a city where food is not just about nourishment but a celebration of culture. Whether you're eating in a high-end restaurant, at a street food stall, or in a local family's home, knowing the dining etiquette will enhance your experience.

Chopsticks: In Shanghai, chopsticks are the primary utensil, and using them properly is essential. When eating, never stick your chopsticks upright into a bowl of rice, as this resembles the incense sticks used in funeral rituals, which is considered disrespectful. Also, avoid pointing or waving your chopsticks around. If you're not using them, place them neatly on the rest provided or across your bowl.

Serving and Sharing: A typical Chinese meal in Shanghai is served family-style, meaning that dishes are shared among everyone at the table. The act of offering food to others before serving yourself is a sign of respect, especially for the elders or guests. When someone offers you food, it's polite to accept, even if you don't particularly want it. Refusing outright can come across as rude.

Tea Etiquette: Tea is an integral part of dining in Shanghai, and the process of pouring tea can be quite formal. It's customary for the youngest person at the table to pour tea for the elders or guests. If someone pours tea for you, gently tap your fingers on the table (a traditional gesture) to thank them, a symbolic way of showing respect.

Toasting: If you're invited to a banquet or celebratory meal, you'll likely encounter the tradition of toasting. "Ganbei" (干杯), which means "Cheers," is commonly heard in Shanghai. When participating in a toast, raise your glass and make eye contact with the person you're toasting to. It's considered polite to take a sip of your drink after toasting. In formal settings, the host or eldest person at the table may make the first toast, and you should follow their lead.

Punctuality: In Chinese culture, punctuality is highly valued. Arriving late to a meal, especially in a formal setting, can be seen as disrespectful. Always try to arrive on time, or even a bit early, to show respect for your host.

Cultural Do's and Don'ts for Visitors

Shanghai is a city where traditional values coexist with modern influences. While the city is progressive and familiar with international visitors, there are still cultural norms that are important to respect. Being mindful of these will help you blend in and show your respect for local customs.

Do Greet with a Smile: A warm and friendly demeanor goes a long way in Shanghai. While handshakes are common in business settings, a polite nod or a slight bow is often used when greeting people in more informal settings. A friendly smile is always appreciated and helps create a welcoming atmosphere.

Don't Engage in Public Displays of Affection: Although Shanghai is a modern city, public displays of affection, such as kissing or hugging, are still considered inappropriate in public, especially in more traditional or conservative settings. Keep your physical interactions more reserved when out in public spaces.

Do Dress Modestly: While Shanghai is a cosmopolitan city with a vibrant fashion scene, it's important to dress appropriately, particularly in temples, religious sites, and formal settings. Revealing clothing may not be well-received, so it's best to dress conservatively when visiting sacred or cultural locations. For example, when visiting temples like the Jade Buddha Temple or the Longhua Temple, covering your shoulders and avoiding overly short clothing is respectful.

Don't Tip: Unlike many Western countries, tipping is not a customary practice in Shanghai. In fact, in most cases, it may be seen as unnecessary or even awkward. Service charges are typically included in restaurant bills, and tipping is not expected. However, if you receive exceptional service, you may offer a small tip, but it's important to be discreet about it. For instance, in high-end hotels or fine dining establishments, tipping is often not required, but rounding up the bill is acceptable in more casual settings.

Do Respect Elders: In Chinese culture, elders are highly respected, and there are several practices to honor them. For instance, when dining, it's customary for younger people to serve older individuals first. If you're in the presence of older people, you should greet them with a respectful address and defer to them in social situations. When visiting family or friends, bringing small gifts for the elders as a sign of respect is also appreciated.

Don't Discuss Sensitive Topics: Shanghai, like the rest of China, has its share of sensitive topics, including politics, religion, and issues surrounding the government. It's advisable to avoid discussing these subjects unless you are in a very familiar setting with people you trust. Political discussions or criticism, particularly about the Chinese government or historical events like Tiananmen Square, can lead to discomfort or even confrontation.

Do Bargain in Markets: If you're shopping in the local markets, especially for souvenirs or clothes, bargaining is a common practice. Many of the vendors expect you to negotiate the price, so it's part of the shopping experience. Start by offering a lower price than the asking price, but always remain polite and friendly throughout the process. Don't be aggressive, as this can cause offense.

Bargaining is much less common in high-end malls or department stores, where prices are fixed.

Don't Overstay Your Welcome: Chinese culture values privacy, and while you may be warmly welcomed into someone's home, it's important to be mindful of not overstaying your visit. If you're invited to someone's home for dinner or tea, a good rule of thumb is to limit your time to a few hours, unless otherwise indicated. Be aware of the host's body language—if they start to clean up or make moves toward ending the evening, it's time to thank them for their hospitality and politely exit.

Do Be Prepared for Quietness: Shanghai's public spaces, especially in transportation hubs and public places like parks and temples, tend to be quieter than what many visitors from Western countries might expect. People generally speak in hushed tones, and public disturbances are frowned upon. In restaurants or public areas, maintain a calm and reserved demeanor. Loud conversations or disruptions are considered impolite.

Made in the USA
Las Vegas, NV
05 April 2025

20578648R00063